# DINOSAURS

## INCREDIBLE BUT TRUE FACTS

This edition published by Parragon Books Ltd in 2015

Parragon Books Ltd
Chartist House
15–17 Trim Street
Bath BA1 1HA, UK
www.parragon.com

English translation edited by Robyn Newton
and Nicola Barber
Consultants: John Cooper and Michael J. Benton
Translated by Elena Horas

ISBN 978-1-4748-1454-6

Printed in China

discovery k!ds™

# DINOSAURS

## INCREDIBLE BUT TRUE FACTS

PaRragon

Bath · New York · Cologne · Melbourne · Delhi
Hong Kong · Shenzhen · Singapore · Amsterdam

# CONTENTS

# Introduction

Ever since the first dinosaur bones were brought to light nearly two hundred years ago, people have been fascinated by these extinct creatures. The term *dinosaur* comes from two Greek words meaning 'terrible lizard'. It was first used in 1842 by the British palaeontologist Sir Richard Owen. Palaeontologists study fossils and other evidence of ancient life to learn about the history of our planet. Every fossil is a clue, and from these clues they can build up a picture of life in prehistoric times.

Our planet was formed around 4600 million years ago. The first living creatures appeared roughly 1200 million years later. These organisms developed from single-celled to multicelled organisms, and they gradually moved from rivers and oceans onto dry land.

The dinosaurs existed during a period of time known as the Mesozoic Era. At first, they lived on the Pangea supercontinent, the only land mass on the planet at that time. Gradually their population increased, and they became extremely varied, until they were the most common form of life on land. Enormous herbivores (plant-eaters) such as *Diplodocus* roamed the land alongside powerful predators such as *Giganotosaurus*. But by the end of the Mesozoic Era, 65 million years ago, there were no dinosaurs left on Earth. Scientists still debate what could have happened to cause this mass extinction.

For a long time, many palaeontologists thought that dinosaurs were slow-moving creatures, with behaviour similar to some reptiles of today. But more recent evidence has suggested that many of the dinosaurs were fast, active creatures that probably lived in groups and travelled long distances. Skin impressions from dinosaurs have also revealed that some of them had feathers. This great discovery was one of the clues that helped to link the dinosaurs with birds.

The study of dinosaurs continues to attract the interest of experts and the public alike. Whatever advances are made in the field of palaeontology, there are always many questions that remain to be answered, and there is always something new to find!

# BEFORE
## THE DINOSAURS

Life on planet Earth started
in the seas and oceans.
Creatures appeared in great
numbers and amazing forms.
As they evolved and adapted
to their surroundings,
life forms gradually began
to appear on land as well.

# Beginning of Life

Scientists divide time into eras in order to talk about events that have happened throughout history and help understand life on Earth. Eras are then divided into periods, epochs and ages to describe shorter amounts of time.

## PRECAMBRIAN ERA

The Precambrian Era spanned more than 4000 million years. Its beginning marked the point when the solid crust of the Earth began to develop from liquid rock, known as lava. Then, around 2100 million years ago, oxygen started to form in the atmosphere.

## PALEOZOIC ERA

The Paleozoic Era started with an explosion of life in the Earth's oceans. It ended with the biggest destruction of species in Earth's history, when nearly 90 per cent of sea life perished. During this era, reptiles, amphibians and insects developed on land.

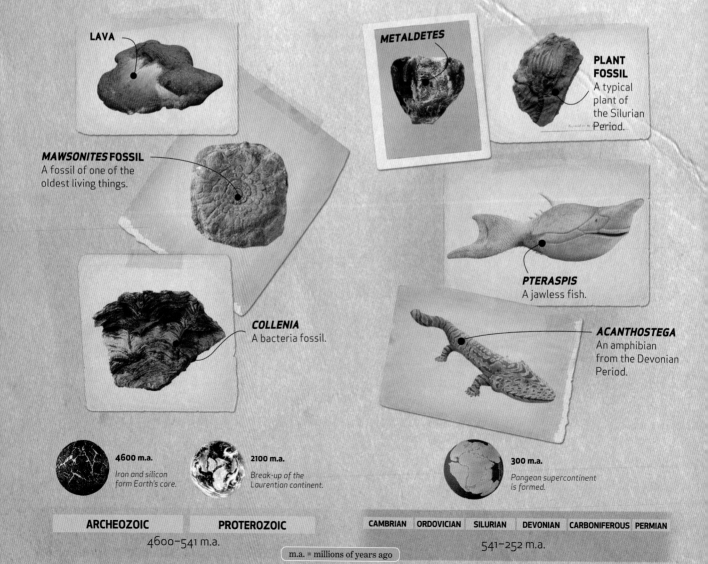

**LAVA**

*MAWSONITES* **FOSSIL**
A fossil of one of the oldest living things.

**COLLENIA**
A bacteria fossil.

*METALDETES*

**PLANT FOSSIL**
A typical plant of the Silurian Period.

*PTERASPIS*
A jawless fish.

*ACANTHOSTEGA*
An amphibian from the Devonian Period.

**4600 m.a.**
*Iron and silicon form Earth's core.*

**2100 m.a.**
*Break-up of the Laurentian continent.*

**300 m.a.**
*Pangean supercontinent is formed.*

| ARCHEOZOIC | PROTEROZOIC |
|---|---|

4600–541 m.a.

| CAMBRIAN | ORDOVICIAN | SILURIAN | DEVONIAN | CARBONIFEROUS | PERMIAN |
|---|---|---|---|---|---|

541–252 m.a.

m.a. = millions of years ago

**4600 m.a.**
Formation of the Earth

**3400 m.a.**
First bacteria (single-celled organisms) appear

**2100 m.a.**
Oxygen forms in the atmosphere

**700 m.a.**
First multicellular animals

PRECAMBRIAN

PALEOZOIC

MESOZOIC

CENOZOIC

## TIMELINE

For the greatest part of history, organisms with only one cell were the main life forms on Earth. The first organisms made up of many cells (multicellular) appeared 700 million years ago.

## MESOZOIC ERA

The Mesozoic Era was the time of the dinosaurs. Other reptiles included tortoises, crocodiles, lizards and snakes. Birds, mammals and the first flowering plants also appeared. The era ended with the disappearance of many life forms.

## CENOZOIC ERA

The dawn of the Cenozoic Era saw the extinction of the dinosaurs. Since then, mammals have dominated, and birds have increased in number. At the very last moment in Earth's long history, human beings appeared.

**BAROSAURUS**
Huge herbivore (plant-eater) that lived 150 million years ago.

**GIGANOTOSAURUS**

**BAROSAURUS BONE**

**TITANIS**
One of the first birds.

**THYLACOSMILUS**
A sabre-toothed marsupial.

**AUSTRALOPITHECUS AFARENSIS**
A human ancestor.

**AUSTRALOPITHECUS**
A human ancestor.

**200–180 m.a.**
*Break-up of Pangea into continents. Africa, India and America separate.*

**60 m.a.**
*Continents are already similar to present-day land masses, and mountains are being formed.*

| TRIASSIC | JURASSIC | CRETACEOUS | | TERTIARY | QUATERNARY |
|----------|----------|------------|--|----------|------------|

252–66 m.a.

From 66 m.a. to present times

# Cambrian Period

Around 541 million years ago, there was an explosion of animal life on Earth. This period is often known as the 'era of the trilobites', because these organisms were found in great numbers in Earth's seas and oceans at that time. Trilobites were arthropods, life forms with hard, jointed coverings. Alongside the trilobites, there were sponges and algae, as well as other invertebrates (animals without a backbone) and the first jawless vertebrates.

**60 cm long**

**SPONGES**
Animals with bodies full of pores (tiny holes). They grew on the seabed. All types of sponges made their appearance in this period, alongside algae.

**PRIAPULIDS**
Sea worms that buried themselves in the sand or mud.

## THE EARTH'S LAND MASSES

During this period, most land masses on Earth were in the Southern Hemisphere. The biggest was Gondwana, which contained the present-day southern continents. Laurentia was second largest in size.

### ANOMALOCARIS
This arthropod was the biggest of the time. It had a round mouth with sharp teeth. It used its spiky outgrowths to capture its prey.

### PIKAIA
Pikaia was one of the first chordates known. A chordate animal has a nerve cord, normally running along its back. This feature first evolved in the early Cambrian Period. Chordates also grew a fish-like tail. Later came the vertebrates, whose nerve cords were protected by a bony spine.

### MARRELLA
An arthropod no more than 2.5 cm long that lived on the seabed.

### HALLUCIGENIA
This unusual creature had spines that it used to move around and to defend itself.

# PALEOZOIC ERA
**CAMBRIAN** ORDOVICIAN  SILURIAN  DEVONIAN  CARBONIFEROUS  PERMIAN

541 m.a.    485 m.a.    444 m.a.    419 m.a.    359 m.a.    299 m.a.

# Ordovician Period

During the second period of the Paleozoic Era, the Ordovician, the number of different life forms increased rapidly, particularly in the seas and oceans. As well as fish, there was a huge range of small invertebrates including bryozoans, trilobites and molluscs. But the period ended with an extinction that killed nearly half of all this sea life.

**BRYOZOANS**
Small invertebrates that looked like plants. Each one was protected by a box-like skeleton.

**CRINOIDS**
Sea lilies attached to the seabed by stalks. Their mouths were surrounded by feeding arms.

**TRILOBITE**
Its body had three segments covered by a hard shell.

## PALEOZOIC ERA

CAMBRIAN **ORDOVICIAN** SILURIAN DEVONIAN CARBONIFEROUS PERMIAN

| 541 m.a. | 485 m.a. | 444 m.a. | 419 m.a. | 359 m.a. | 299 m.a. |

**2.5 M**
**long**

### THE EARTH'S LAND MASSES

During this period, Gondwana moved towards the South Pole. A large part of the continent was underwater.

**NAUTILOIDS**
It is thought that nautiloids were one of the largest animals in this period. They had several arms with a mouth in the middle.

**CORALS**
Together with sponges, crinoids and other animals, corals formed large reefs.

**GASTROPODS**
Similar to present-day snails and slugs, these molluscs moved along the seabed. They fed on small algae and sponges.

# Silurian Period

Plants had already started to grow on land by the beginning of the Silurian Period – mosses and other small plants near coasts, lakes and streams. Invertebrate animals also began to move out of the oceans, but most animal life was still underwater. During this period, bony fish with movable jaws made their appearance.

**JAEKELOPTERUS**
The biggest arthropod known so far, this marine scorpion was a hunter in the sea and in fresh water. Its flat body was protected by a hard covering with flexible joints.

2.5m
**long**

## PALEOZOIC ERA

CAMBRIAN  ORDOVICIAN  **SILURIAN**  DEVONIAN  CARBONIFEROUS  PERMIAN

| 541 m.a. | 485 m.a. | 444 m.a. | 419 m.a. | 359 m.a. | 299 m.a. |

## THE EARTH'S LANDMASSES

Some parts of Gondwana shifted towards the Equator. They gathered in two supercontinents called Laurussia (or Euramerica) and Laurasia. An ice melt caused rises and falls in the sea level.

### *PORASPIS*

One of the jawless fish that appeared during this period. It was covered by a bony shell that helped it to move freely.

### EYES

The eyes were divided into tiny sections, like those of many modern arthropods.

### LEGS

The marine scorpion walked along the seabed on its four pairs of limbs. The pair of limbs behind the legs became flattened like paddles to help the creature swim.

### CLAWS

Very sharp, they were the ideal tools to capture prey.

# Devonian Period

The Devonian Period is often called the 'era of the fish' because of the wide range and huge numbers of fish that swam in the seas and oceans. Armoured fish, such as placoderms, with hard plates on their heads and parts of their bodies, became top hunters. Lungfish and the first amphibians also made their appearance.

**DUNKLEOSTEUS**
This huge placoderm was one of the fiercest predators of the period. It was heavily armoured and weighed up to 4 tonnes.

9 m
**long**

**PTERASPIS**

*Pteraspis* was a jawless fish with a round body. It was covered by plates on its front and had scales on its tail. It fed on small invertebrates.

**TAIL**
The massive tail was thick and pointed at the end.

**BLADES**
*Dunkleosteus* did not have teeth. Instead it used long bony blades on the edges of its jaws to crush prey. It had one of the most powerful bites of any fish ever to have existed.

**THE EARTH'S LAND MASSES**

The supercontinents, Gondwana and Euramerica, gathered together in the Southern Hemisphere. The rest of the globe was covered by water!

# PALEOZOIC ERA

CAMBRIAN  ORDOVICIAN  SILURIAN  **DEVONIAN**  CARBONIFEROUS  PERMIAN

| 541 m.a. | 485 m.a. | 444 m.a. | 419 m.a. | 359 m.a. | 299 m.a. |

# Carboniferous Period

During the Carboniferous Period, oxygen levels on Earth were at their maximum. This, together with a climate warmer than ever before, allowed gigantic insects to evolve. Amphibians began to lose their fish-like appearance, and the first reptiles emerged. The seas and oceans were full of sharks of different varieties.

**HELICOPRION**
This shark-like animal had teeth that formed a strange shape, like a circular saw. *Helicoprion* probably measured 3–4 m in length.

**MEGANEURA**
This truly gigantic dragonfly had wings nearly 76 cm long, *Meganeura* hunted insects and amphibians.

**LIMBS**
The legs of *Acanthostega* were more suitable for moving through water than walking on land.

## THE EARTH'S LAND MASSES

The supercontinent Pangea was formed during this period. The single ocean that surrounded it was called Panthalassa.

### AMNIOTIC EGG

As tetrapods (vertebrates with four limbs) developed during the Carboniferous Period, they became less dependent on water. One change was the development of their eggs, which became covered by a hard shell. Inside, the embryo grew in a cavity full of liquid. This meant that the eggs could be laid and hatched on land.

### ACANTHOSTEGA

This vertebrate spent its time mostly in water (like a fish), but had four recognizable legs (like a land animal). It had a tail fin and it breathed through gills.

**60 cm**
**long**

## PALEOZOIC ERA

CAMBRIAN  ORDOVICIAN  SILURIAN  DEVONIAN  **CARBONIFEROUS**  PERMIAN

541 m.a.  485 m.a.  444 m.a.  419 m.a.  359 m.a.  299 m.a.

# Permian Period

In the Permian Period, a wide range of strange and wonderful species of reptile roamed the Earth. Among them were the ancestors of mammals. A great variety of insects also existed, and bony fish dominated the seas. But, at the end of the period, there was the biggest destruction of all life forms that has ever taken place!

*ESTEMMENOSUCHUS*
This large, clumsy-looking reptile was the size of a bull.

4.5 m
long

PALEOZOIC ERA

CAMBRIAN ORDOVICIAN SILURIAN DEVONIAN CARBONIFEROUS **PERMIAN**

| 541 m.a. | 485 m.a. | 444 m.a. | 419 m.a. | 359 m.a. | 299 m.a. |

## THE EARTH'S LAND MASSES

At the beginning of the Permian Period, the Pangea supercontinent contained most of Earth's land masses and stretched from the South Pole to the North Pole. The rest of the planet was covered by an ocean, called Panthalassa, and Tethys, a small sea.

## STRANGE SKULL

The skull of *Estemmenosuchus* measured about 60 cm in length and had horns that pointed upwards and outwards.

## *LYCOSUCHUS*

One of the main carnivores of the Permian Period, *Lycosuchus* had large canine (long, pointed) teeth.

# Dimetrodon

*Dimetrodon* is often mistaken for a dinosaur but, in fact, it was the most ferocious predator of the early Permian Period, many millions of years before the dinosaurs appeared. It was a type of reptile and an ancient ancestor of primitive mammals.

The name *Dimetrodon* means 'two measures of teeth', and it did indeed have two kinds of very sharp teeth! Small teeth on both sides of the mouth and larger teeth on the front of the snout helped *Dimetrodon* to tear flesh off its prey.

This carnivorous reptile lived in the early Permian Period. Its most eye-catching feature was the large 'sail' on its back – a structure of delicate bones, connected by thick, hard skin.

During the 50 million years of the Permian Period, different species of vertebrates appeared one after another on land. It was at the beginning of the period that sphenacodontids – ancient carnivorous reptiles such as *Dimetrodon* – developed.

In the Late Permian, it was mammal-like reptiles that dominated. They included both flesh-eating species, such as gorgonopsids, and plant-eating species, such as dicynodonts. The end of the Permian Period saw a great variety of animal life, ranging from small carnivores to the huge herbivorous species found in the Karoo rocks of South Africa.

In 2001, a new species of *Dimetrodon* was found in Germany, extending its geographic range even further.

GENUS: DIMETRODON
CLASSIFICATION: SYNAPSIDA, SPHENACODONTIDAE

LENGTH 3 m
WEIGHT 250 kg
DIET Carnivorous

**LOCATION**
*Dimetrodon* fossils have been found in rocks 270 million years old in the United States.

Many species of the Middle and Later Permian Period have been found in South Africa and Russia.

**SAIL SPINES**
The spines extended upwards in a grill shape, connected by hard skin.

# Dimetrodon

## POSTURE

The legs of *Dimetrodon* spread out from its sides, like those of a lizard, so that its belly dragged when it walked slowly. But, when hunting, this posture may have helped *Dimetrodon* to run faster.

## PHYLOGENETIC TREE

The Phylogenetic Tree, or Evolutionary Tree, is a diagram showing the relationships between species from common ancestors. Look at the tree on each new species page to see when the species evolved.

| CARBONIFEROUS | PERMIAN | TRIASSIC | JURASSIC | CRETACEOUS |
|---|---|---|---|---|
| 299 m.a. | 252 m.a. | 201 m.a. | 145 m.a. | 66 m.a. |

Sphenacodontids

Mammals

Synapsids

Cynodonts

Amniotes

Therocephalians

Reptiles

**SKELETON**
The skeleton shows the spines clearly.

**EDAPHOSAURUS**
This herbivorous reptile lived at the same time as *Dimetrodon*. It also had a huge sail, possibly to control the temperature of its body.

**RITUAL FIGHT**
*Dimetrodon*'s sail may have played an important role in attracting mates, as well as frightening rivals.

**LOOKING FORWARD TO THE DINOSAURS**
Many dinosaurs, pterosaurs and crocodiles evolved from small reptiles that looked like lizards and lived in the Permian Period.

**FEET**
*Dimetrodon* had five short toes with small but sharp claws on each.

# Dimetrodon

**SKULL**
Behind *Dimetrodon*'s eyes, there were holes in the skull for muscles that controlled the mouth. These strong muscles would have given *Dimetrodon* a powerful jaw.

**PRIMITIVE LEGS**
These front legs might have been used for holding and tearing prey.

**SAIL**
It's possible that the sail worked as a kind of temperature controller. At dawn the animal would have faced towards the sun to get warm. At midday the sail would have provided shade to avoid *Dimetrodon* overheating.

**LETHAL TAIL**
*Dimetrodon*'s tail was long and strong. It was made up of bulky muscles, so it could be used as a weapon.

# SPECIES
## OF DINOSAURS

At the end of the Triassic Period, the dinosaurs took over from the reptiles that dominated our planet previously. They developed into many different shapes and sizes and ruled the Earth.

# What is a Dinosaur?

Dinosaurs were reptiles that appeared about 230 million years ago. They evolved into an amazing variety of shapes and types: some were giants, others small; some herbivores, others carnivores. They had horns, crests, bony plates and even feathers as protection. The dinosaurs disappeared in the Cretaceous Period but left behind descendants that could fly and had feathers – birds!

**D**inosaurs looked different from tortoises, lizards or crocodiles because of their body posture. Their limbs came downwards from their bodies, not out from their sides, as in most reptiles. Their posture was straighter, and they were able to move faster and more gracefully than other reptiles. Dinosaurs could rise onto their rear legs and use their toes when walking or running. This more efficient way of moving was one of the keys to the dinosaurs' success against the competition of other reptilian species.

Many dinosaur species reached gigantic sizes. *Argentinosaurus* and *Puertasaurus* are considered the largest land animals ever. They reached lengths of almost 35 metres from the tip of the nose to the end of the tail. But not all dinosaurs were huge. There were some dinosaurs the same size as chickens, such as *Scipionyx* from Italy, *Microraptor* from China and *Ligabueino* from Argentina.

**TAIL**
A long and robust tail was used to balance the weight of the body.

**NECK**
This part of the body became S-shaped.

**LEGS**
The structure of the legs and hips was similar to that of present-day birds.

## THE EVOLUTION OF REPTILES

As dinosaurs evolved from reptiles, the main changes were related to movement, from reptilian to bipedal (two-footed) forms.

**1 REPTILIAN**

In lizards, the limbs spread outwards, with elbows and knees bending, and the belly dragging on the ground.

**2 SEMI-ERECT**

In crocodiles, the limbs stretch outwards and downwards, with elbows and knees bent at an angle of 45 degrees. Crocodiles crawl when moving slowly and straighten their legs when running.

**3 BIPEDS**

In dinosaurs, the rear limbs were straight beneath the body, so that the body was never dragged, not even when the dinosaur was walking very slowly.

# Classification

This chart shows the relationships between the groups of dinosaurs, starting from the main divisions (Saurischia and Ornithischia) when they first evolved from early reptiles in the Triassic Period. Over the next 160 million years they evolved into many different groups.

Prosauropoda — Plateosaurus, Massospondylus

Sauropodomorpha

Eoraptor

Herrerasaurus

Isanosaurus — Sauropoda

Allosauroidea — Cryolophosaurus, Allosaurus, Piatnitzkysaurus

Saurischia

Coelophysis — Theropoda

DINOSAURIA

Liliensternus

Compsognathus

Ornitholestes

Ornithischia

Ceratosaurus

Marginocephalia

Ornithopoda

Stegosauria — Stegosaurus, Tuojiangosaurus

Thyreophora

Scelidosaurus — Ankylosauria

## MESOZOIC ERA

**TRIASSIC** Dinosaurs appeared in this period, 235 million years ago. They lived alongside other reptiles.

**JURASSIC 150 m.a.** Gigantic herbivores appeared, along with powerful carnivores. At the end of this period, the first birds developed.

Laurasia

Gondwana

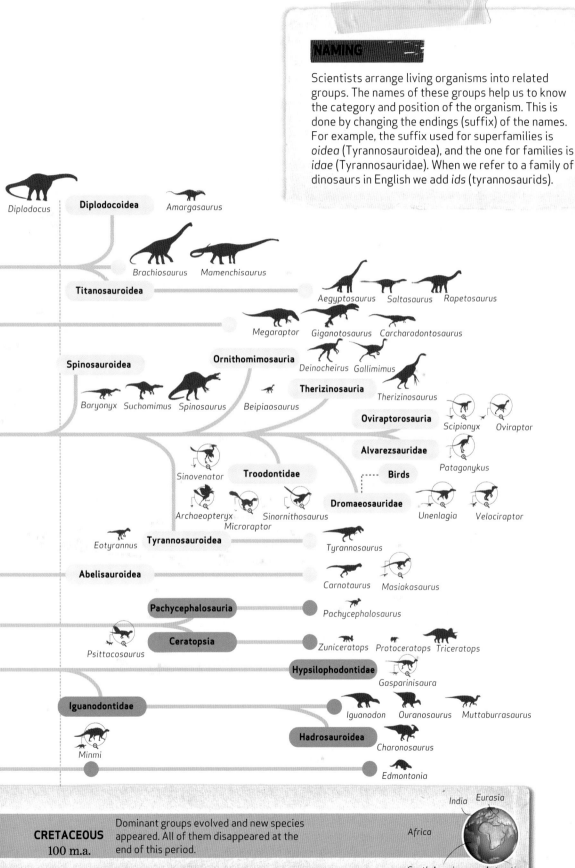

**NAMING**

Scientists arrange living organisms into related groups. The names of these groups help us to know the category and position of the organism. This is done by changing the endings (suffix) of the names. For example, the suffix used for superfamilies is *oidea* (Tyrannosauroidea), and the one for families is *idae* (Tyrannosauridae). When we refer to a family of dinosaurs in English we add *ids* (tyrannosaurids).

Diplodocus

**Diplodocoidea**

Amargasaurus

Brachiosaurus    Mamenchisaurus

**Titanosauroidea**

Aegyptosaurus    Saltasaurus    Rapetosaurus

Megaraptor    Giganotosaurus    Carcharodontosaurus

**Spinosauroidea**

**Ornithomimosauria**

Deinocheirus    Gallimimus

Baryonyx    Suchomimus    Spinosaurus

Beipiaosaurus

**Therizinosauria**

Therizinosaurus

**Oviraptorosauria**

Scipionyx    Oviraptor

**Alvarezsauridae**

Patagonykus

**Troodontidae**

Sinovenator

**Birds**

**Dromaeosauridae**

Unenlagia    Velociraptor

Archaeopteryx    Sinornithosaurus
Microraptor

Eotyrannus

**Tyrannosauroidea**

Tyrannosaurus

**Abelisauroidea**

Carnotaurus    Masiakasaurus

**Pachycephalosauria**

Pachycephalosaurus

**Ceratopsia**

Psittacosaurus

Zuniceratops    Protoceratops    Triceratops

**Hypsilophodontidae**

Gasparinisaura

**Iguanodontidae**

Iguanodon    Ouranosaurus    Muttaburrasaurus

Minmi

**Hadrosauroidea**

Charonosaurus

Edmontonia

India    Eurasia

Africa

South America    Antarctica

**CRETACEOUS**
**100 m.a.**

Dominant groups evolved and new species appeared. All of them disappeared at the end of this period.

# Tyrannosaurus rex

*Tyrannosaurus rex* had a huge head, strong and sharp teeth, and legs well suited for running. This dinosaur was one of the most extraordinary creatures of the prehistoric world!

Tyrannosaurus rex and its close relatives, the tyrannosaurids, evolved in the Northern Hemisphere in the late Cretaceous Period. Skeletons, teeth and footprints of these carnivores have been found in North America and Central Asia.

They were great hunters. Their favourite prey included ceratopsians and hadrosaurs. The larger tyrannosaurids lived alongside the dromaeosaurids (small-sized, fast-running carnivorous dinosaurs).

The strength of *Tyrannosaurus* lay in its huge jaws, powered by muscles in its temples. The shape of the skull hints that it had a good sense of smell, which helped it to find prey.

There have been many different theories about the feeding habits of *Tyrannosaurus*. It was once thought that it was unable to hunt successfully! But this may not be true. Its hind legs show that it would have been able to pick up enough speed to hunt heavy animals that could not run as fast. Skeletons of *Triceratops* and other hadrosaurs have been found with large teeth marks, thought to have been made by tyrannosaurids. This clue leads us to believe that *Tyrannosaurus* would have been able to capture its prey alive. However, during long periods of drought, it was likely to have scavenged for leftovers.

GENUS: TYRANNOSAURUS
CLASSIFICATION: THEROPODA, COELUROSAURIA, TYRANNOSAURIDAE

**LENGTH** 12.5 m
**WEIGHT** 5000 kg
**DIET** Carnivorous

**TERRIBLE TEETH**
*Tyrannosaurus* teeth were big enough to crunch bones. They could be up to 30 centimetres long!

The arms were tiny – about the same length as a human's arms, with two small fingers on the end. They were too small and short to be used to capture prey.

**POWERFUL FEET**
Each foot had three strong toes, used to force prey against the ground. There was also a fourth toe, called a dewclaw, higher on the foot, but this was almost useless.

**LOCATION**
*Tyrannosaurus rex* fossils have been found in the United States and Canada, along with other tyrannosaurids, including *Daspletosaurus*, *Gorgosaurus* and *Albertosaurus*.

Tyrannosaurid fossils have even been found on the other side of the world in Asia, including that of *Guanlong*, a primitive tyrannosaurid from the Jurassic Period.

# Tyrannosaurus rex

**FEROCIOUS TEETH**
The teeth were rounded and pointed, not blade-shaped as in other theropods.

**NAMING *TYRANNOSAURUS***
In 1905, Henry Fairfield Osborn, a palaeontologist at the American Museum of Natural History in New York, United States, came up with the name *Tyrannosaurus rex*.

*PHYLOGENETIC TREE*

| PERMIAN | 252 m.a. | TRIASSIC | 201 m.a. | JURASSIC | 145 m.a. | CRETACEOUS | 66 m.a. |
|---|---|---|---|---|---|---|---|
| | | | | Coelosaurs | | Tyrannosaurids | |
| | | | | | | | |
| | | Tetanurans | | | | | |
| | | | | | | | |
| Theropods | | | | | | | |

**SKELETON**
The skeleton of *Tyrannosaurus rex* is believed to have around 200 bones.

**PADDED FEET**
*Tyrannosaurus'* three main toes had sharp claws. Underneath, they were padded to absorb impact against the ground.

# Tyrannosaurus rex

**FEATHERED BABY**
A baby *Tyrannosaurus rex* probably had feathers, and many scientists think adults might have, too.

**BIG HUNTER**
It is thought that, due to its strength, *Tyrannosaurus* could bring down large herbivores.

**LEGS**
*Tyrannosaurus'* legs were long and muscular. Despite their weight, some scientists believe that these huge dinosaurs could still run to chase their prey.

**HUGE HEAD**
The head was 1.4 m in length, and it had between 50 and 60 teeth in total.

**ARMS**
They were so small that *Tyrannosaurus* couldn't even reach its own mouth!

# Anatomy Characteristics

Fossils of dinosaur skeletons, teeth, footprints, eggs and skin have given us huge amounts of information about the different kinds of dinosaurs. Palaeontologists piece this information together with data about the dinosaurs' environment and present-day species to build up a picture of the anatomy (body structure) of dinosaurs.

We know from the many fossilized dinosaur skeletons found that dinosaurs looked very similar to other reptiles. Bone structure, the scales that covered their bodies and their birth from shelled eggs are key similarities.

Dinosaurs, however, had many features that were different from their reptile relatives, such as adaptations in their legs and hips, as they developed from crawling to an upright posture. During this process, a new arrangement of muscles evolved.

Most of the information we have about the body structure of dinosaurs comes from their bones, as these hard parts fossilized best. In a very few cases, impressions (marks on a surface) of dinosaur skin have been found. From these we know that some dinosaurs had hard coverings and small scales, while some recently discovered dinosaurs had feathery coverings. The study of present-day birds and reptiles also helps us to reconstruct the body posture of dinosaurs.

Ossified tendons (flexible cords that have changed into bone-like material)

Tibia (shin bone)

### DEINONYCHUS SKELETON

The main features of the carnivorous dinosaur *Deinonychus* were similar to those of other theropods: a large skull, a short and curved neck, a strong backbone and hind legs much longer than the front ones.

Deltoid (thick triangular muscle across the shoulder joint)

Scapular muscle

Iliotibial band

**MUSCLES**

With the help of the stretch marks, depressions (hollows) and crests found on dinosaur bones, we can identify the positions of muscles in the body.

Gastrocnemius (largest muscle of the leg)

Triceps

Extensor digitorum longus (muscle on the front of the leg that extends to the toes)

Abdominal muscle

Sacral vertebrae (bones in the lower back)

Femur (thigh bone)

Cranial cavity (hollow space in the skull of a vertebrate)

Cervical vertebrae (bones in the neck area)

**INSIDE THE BONES**
The study of the inside of dinosaur bones (osseous tissue) gives hints about how the bones grew.

Sickle-shaped claw

Phalanx (bones of the fingers or toes)

# Inside a Dinosaur

## CENTRAL CONTROL

The brains of herbivores were smaller than the brains of carnivores. A dinosaur's brain was located and protected inside the skull, just like ours, and different nerves pointed outwards to collect information from the eyes, nose, mouth and ear openings. The spinal cord started from the brain and extended through the backbone.

Kidney

Small intestine

Lung

Heart

Liver

Large intestine

## INTERNAL ORGANS

In the biggest herbivorous dinosaurs (the sauropods), the thorax (the middle region of the body between the head and the stomach) was so large that an adult African elephant would have fitted into it! The heart was as big as a barrel and was located inside the thorax along with the lungs.

## SIZE AND WEIGHT

Dinosaurs were the group of reptiles with the widest range of sizes. Some dinosaurs, such as *Epidexipteryx*, were as tiny as sparrows. Others, including *Argentinosaurus*, were as big as blue whales!

**SIZE**
Many dinosaurs were small in size.

Basset hound

Velociraptor

**WEIGHT COMPARISON**
1 African elephant (5400 kg) = 15 *Protoceratops*

**SIZE COMPARISON**

### STEGOSAURUS
Stegosaurus had a brain the size of a walnut.

### TYRANNOSAURUS
Tyrannosaurus had a brain smaller than that of humans.

### TROODON
Troodon's brain was similar in size to that of Tyrannosaurus rex, but because it was large in relation to its head, it is thought to have been a more intelligent dinosaur.

Cloaca (reproductive and excretory opening)

Caecum (secondary digestion chamber to further break down food in order for the dinosaur to get essential nutrients from the plants it ate)

Muscular stomach

1 Tyrannosaurus rex (5000 kg) = 1 African elephant

1 Argentinosaurus (73,000 kg) = 17 African elephants

# Mesozoic Era

The 185-million-year span of the Mesozoic Era is divided into three periods: Triassic, Jurassic and Cretaceous. Dinosaurs were the most famous members of this era, which is often called 'the era of the reptiles'. But dinosaurs only began to appear at the end of the Triassic Period, taking the place of the ancient reptiles.

The start of the Mesozoic Era, around 250 million years ago, saw the extinction of huge numbers of the species that had inhabited Earth during the previous Paleozoic Era. The creatures that did survive the extinction were sea dwellers. These included amniotes (four-legged creatures with backbones that lay eggs) and molluscs.

During the Mesozoic Era itself, many organisms, including plants, invertebrates and vertebrates, appeared and grew in number. In the seas, gigantic reptiles, such as ichthyosaurs and plesiosaurs, fed on all types of fish. On the coasts and dry land, crocodiles, salamanders and other reptiles grew in number and variety. In the middle of the Mesozoic Era, dinosaurs began to make their appearance. Towards the end of the Triassic, as many other reptiles became extinct, the dinosaurs began to rule the Earth.

**VEGETATION**
Gigantic conifers (cone-bearing trees) developed.

*Pangea*

**THE EARTH'S LAND MASSES**

At the beginning of the Mesozoic Era, the continental masses were gathered into a supercontinent, called Pangea. During the Late Triassic, Pangea began to separate into an upper part (Laurasia) and a lower one (Gondwana), divided by the Tethys Sea.

**INVERTEBRATES**
Grasshoppers appeared, and spiders and scorpions grew in number.

**TRIASSIC LANDSCAPE**
Red beds of sandstone made for a very dry environment, where the earliest dinosaurs evolved.

**NUMEROUS SPECIES**
Alongside the dinosaurs, reptiles and mammals grew in number.

**PLANTS**
Pangea was a warm desert, where conifers, palm trees and smaller plants, such as ginkgos and cycads, grew. Some plants from this era, such as ferns, have survived to modern times.

*Leptocycas gigas* (cycad from the end of the Triassic)

**ANIMALS**
Ancestors of the dinosaurs, such as *Lagosuchus*, and the dinosaurs themselves, lived in many parts of the world during the Triassic Period.

# The Ischigualasto Formation

Around 228 million years ago, in the south of Gondwana, the first dinosaurs lived alongside the last therapsids (mammal-like reptiles). The remains of these and other reptiles, together with amphibians, invertebrates and plants, have been uncovered as fossils.

The Ischigualasto Provincial Park is one of the most important fossil sites of the Mesozoic Era. Also known as the 'Valley of the Moon' because of its desert landscape, it is located in San Juan, in the north-west of Argentina. It shows layers of rocky deposits from the entire 50 million years of the Triassic Period that give us a unique fossil record of the period.

The first fossils found in Ischigualasto were collected in 1942. As well as dinosaur fossils, the Formation includes reptile fossils. These support the theory that the dinosaurs and ancestors of mammals appeared gradually at the same time, and other reptiles then began to disappear.

Study of the rocks has revealed that the climate was extremely dry in the Early Triassic. However, during the middle of the Triassic the air was more humid, as many plants and animals have been preserved in the rock. Later, volcanic activity spread ashes which helped to preserve animal and plant life as fossils.

*DICROIDIUM*
*Dicroidium* was one of the most common plants in the Ischigualasto Formation. It grew among low-growing plants in forests and on flooded plains. It formed part of the green and bushy habitats of the Middle Triassic.

Early Triassic     Middle Triassic     Late Triassic

Dry environment     Vegetable remains     Dinosaurs

**CARNIVORE OR OMNIVORE?**
The small and fast-moving saurischian dinosaur *Eoraptor* might have been a carnivore (meat-eater) or an omnivore (plant- and meat-eater).

**GIANT HERBIVORE**
*Ischigualastia* was a massive, hippo-sized herbivorous therapsid.

**TINY DINOSAUR**
*Pisanosaurus* was a small ornithischian dinosaur, rare in the Triassic.

# Dinosaur Ancestors

The Ischigualasto Formation has given us information about the oldest known species of dinosaurs. Fossils of *Herrerasaurus ischigualastensis* and *Eoraptor lunensis* that were found at Ischigualasto date back between 230 and 218 million years. From these and other fossils found in the Formation, we have learned about the evolution of dinosaurs.

Ischigualasto has revealed fossils from the ancestors of birds, crocodiles and lizards. Thousands of specimens have been collected, including the remains of the earliest dinosaur, *Eoraptor lunensis,* and its more advanced relative, the carnivorous *Herrerasaurus ischigualastensis.*

Most of the fossils have been found in the top levels of the Formation and consist almost entirely of archosaurs. Archosaurs included the earliest ancestors of present-day crocodiles. *Saurosuchus galilei* was a type of archosaur known as a rauisuchian. It was a speedy carnivore that moved in a similar way to the crocodiles we know today. *Sillosuchus longicervix* was also discovered in Ischigualasto.

Its name comes from the Greek word *suchus,* meaning 'crocodile'.

## SILLOSUCHUS LONGICERVIX

Related to present-day crocodiles, *Sillosuchus* had two long legs and lived on land. Its skeleton was light, which helped it to move fast.

**ALL SIZES**

The reptiles at Ischigualasto came in a wide variety of sizes. *Ischigualastia* was the size of a cow. There were also smaller forms, such as *Probainognathus*, which had a skull length of just 2 cm! Many of the fossils at Ischigualasto reveal supersized animals. *Saurosuchus*, an ancestor of the crocodiles, was almost 6 m long. Of the dinosaurs, *Herrerasaurus* was the largest, with a body length of more than 3 m.

Aetosauroides

Hyperodapedon

Herrerasaurus

Ischigualastia

Saurosuchus

Sillosuchus

Exaeretodon

Eoraptor

Ecteninion

Venaticosuchus

Probelesodon

Proterochampsa

Probainognathus

**VALLEY OF CROCODILES**
More than a dozen ancient crocodiles have been found at Ischigualasto, belonging to the Middle and Late Triassic.

**MEAT-EATER**
The largest carnivorous therapsid, *Chinicuodon theotonicus*, is known only from the remains of its skull.

# Herrerasaurus

*Herrerasaurus* was a fast-moving carnivore that was well adapted for hunting other herbivorous and omnivorous reptiles. Its remains have helped to provide important information about the origin and varied forms of dinosaurs.

Herrerasaurus was one of the earliest known dinosaurs to be discovered, alongside others, such as *Eoraptor*, *Panphagia* and *Staurikosaurus*. They were all found in rocks from the Triassic Period, dating back approximately 228 million years.

Compared to reptiles at that time, *Herrerasaurus* was a rare species! It is classified as a saurischian theropod (a reptile-hipped dinosaur that was two-legged). It was one of the earliest meat-eating dinosaurs, with teeth of different sizes and shapes. The largest were very sharp and allowed *Herrerasaurus* to catch and kill prey. It also had big jaws, curved and pointed claws, and it could move at great speed. These features made it one of the most powerful hunters of the time.

GENUS: HERRERASAURUS
CLASSIFICATION: DINOSAURIA, THEROPODA, HERRERASAURIDAE

LENGTH 3 m
WEIGHT 210 kg
DIET Carnivorous

## SKELETON

The skeleton of *Herrerasaurus* had a mixture of characteristics, some of which were similar to early reptiles, such as the two bones in its hip. Others were more advanced, dinosaur-like features, such as its ankle bones.

## SHORT ARMS

The arms of *Herrerasaurus* were relatively short and are similar to those of later carnivorous dinosaurs. They had powerful claws to capture their prey.

## LOCATION

*Herrerasaurus* was found in the Ischigualasto Provincial Park, in north-west Argentina. Remains of *Staurikosaurus* and *Sanjuansaurus*, also in the herrerasaurid family, have been found in the same place.

# Herrerasaurus

In 1961, a team of explorers carried out a study in Ischigualasto. One of the team, Victorino Herrer, together with a local rancher and a collector, found a leg, a part of a hip and most of the tail bones of a dinosaur. They also discovered many fragments of bones that belonged to the same species. From these remains, an Argentinian palaeontologist, Osvaldo Reig, was able to describe *Herrerasaurus ischigualastensis*. He named it after its discoverer and the place it was found.

*Herrerasaurus* is now considered an 'ancestral species' because it lived at a time when dinosaurs were still evolving. Its skeleton shows features midway between these early reptiles and fully developed dinosaurs. It could run on two legs, unlike its ancestors, and so its arms and hands developed into efficient prey-grabbing tools, just like many later dinosaurs.

### COMPARING ANCESTORS

As well as *Herrerasaurus*, *Eoraptor* and *Pisanosaurus* were the other ancient animals of this time. They have all been the subject of much debate in attempting to place them on the evolutionary tree of the dinosaurs.

### HIND LEGS

The structure of *Herrerasaurus'* hind legs was very similar to its reptile ancestors.

## PHYLOGENETIC TREE

| PERMIAN | | TRIASSIC | | JURASSIC | | CRETACEOUS | |
|---------|---|----------|---|----------|---|------------|---|
| | 252 m.a. | | 201 m.a. | | 145 m.a. | | 66 m.a. |

Archosaurs

Saurischians

Theropods

Hyperodapedon

Exaeretodon

**POSSIBLE PREY**

*Herrerasaurus* hunted therapsids such as *Hyperodapedon* and the slow-moving *Exaeretodon*. It might also have hunted smaller dinosaurs, such as *Eoraptor*, as well as amphibians and large insects of the Triassic.

**JAW MOVEMENT**
*Herrerasaurus'* jaws had a special joint that allowed them flexible movement to grasp their prey.

**CLAWS**
The claws on each finger were very sharp.

# Herrerasaurus

**MOVEMENT**
*Herrerasaurus* had legs adapted for long strides. When running, its tail stuck out straight to balance the front of its body.

**RECONSTRUCTION**
The first complete jointed skeleton of *Herrerasaurus* was found in 1992. Before that date, it had been reconstructed from different pieces collected from different specimens.

**MOUTH**
*Herrerasaurus* had large jaws with many saw-like teeth that curved backwards. These were specially adapted to its carnivorous diet.

**FINGERS**
The physical features of *Herrerasaurus'* legs and hands, such as the outer fingers, were the same as those of ancient theropod dinosaurs.

# Jurassic Period

The Jurassic Period was the time when the biggest living creatures ever seen on Earth roamed the planet. There were many different reptiles that lived on the land, in the sea and in the sky. Large herbivorous and smaller carnivorous dinosaurs dominated the land.

D inosaurs grew to huge sizes in the Jurassic Period. Sauropods (plant-eating dinosaurs), such as *Diplodocus* and *Brachiosaurus,* were among the largest. Other herbivorous species, such as the stegosaurs, developed fearsome body protection to fight large, powerful carnivores.

Alongside the larger dinosaurs were smaller, faster species that may have hunted in groups. *Archaeopteryx*, the first known bird, appeared towards the end of the Jurassic. It shared the skies with flying reptiles that had been on the planet since the Triassic.

In the oceans, ichthyosaurs and plesiosaurs lived with big sea crocodiles, sharks, rays and various cephalopods (molluscs with tentacles, such as octopuses), which were similar to those alive today!

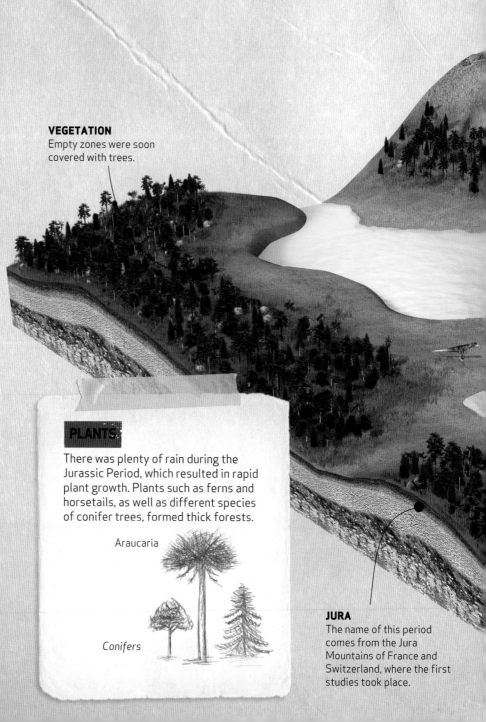

**VEGETATION**
Empty zones were soon covered with trees.

**PLANTS**

There was plenty of rain during the Jurassic Period, which resulted in rapid plant growth. Plants such as ferns and horsetails, as well as different species of conifer trees, formed thick forests.

Araucaria

Conifers

**JURA**
The name of this period comes from the Jura Mountains of France and Switzerland, where the first studies took place.

**JURASSIC LANDSCAPE**
A warm, wet climate gave rise to lush vegetation and abundant life. Many new dinosaurs emerged in great numbers.

**ORNITHISCHIANS**
Ornithischian (bird-hipped) dinosaurs were found in great numbers.

Laurasia          Gondwana

**THE EARTH'S LAND MASSES**

North America moved towards the north and separated from what is now South America. North America, together with Europe and part of Asia, formed Laurasia, although Europe was covered by shallow waters. In the south, the Antarctic, South America, India and Australia formed Gondwana.

**ANIMALS**

Herbivorous dinosaurs, such as *Brachiosaurus*, and carnivores, such as *Allosaurus*, dominated the land.

*Allosaurus*

**COAL**
Many deposits of coal date from this period.

# The Morrison Formation

Situated in the western United States, the Morrison Formation is one of the most amazing fossil sites in the world. Thousands of fossil remains of some of the best-known Jurassic dinosaurs have been found here.

The Morrison Formation is made up of rocks that were deposited over a span of eight million years in the Late Jurassic Period. The first fossils were uncovered in 1877, and remarkable dinosaurs, such as *Stegosaurus, Diplodocus, Brachiosaurus* and *Allosaurus,* were discovered.

We have also been able to find out that, in the Late Jurassic, the climate in this region was warm and mostly dry. Rivers often dried up completely, but they could also flood suddenly after rainfall. Alongside the rivers grew low, soft plants, such as ferns, as well as trees. In the lakes and rivers, there were many varieties of fish and invertebrates, such as crabs, snails and clams.

Frogs, lizards, tortoises and crocodiles lived around the lakes. Pterosaurs (flying reptiles) searched for fish and the first mammals also appeared here.

Among the many discoveries in the Morrison Formation was a fossil footprint trail. This is the longest ever found, at about 4 kilometres in length!

**HUGE DINOSAURS**
From the fossils found in the Morrison Formation, we know that sauropods reached their maximum size in this region. This may have been due to seasonal rains and the resulting increased availability of sources of food, such as plants and trees.

ORIGINS
These rocks were formed by deposits on an enclosed area of water in the west of Pangea. The constantly changing environment, with frequent river flooding and droughts, helped to fossilize bones.

**FOSSIL WARS**
At the end of the 19th century, the Morrison Formation had its own 'bone wars', as palaeontologists Othniel C. Marsh and Edward D. Cope competed for the discovery of the largest number of fossils!

**NATURAL MONUMENT**
One enormous block of rocks contains around 1500 fossilized bones, exactly as they were buried 150 million years ago during a river flood!

**DROUGHT**
The Jurassic environment could, at times, become extremely dry. In these extreme conditions, vegetation would have died out first, followed by the herbivorous dinosaurs and then by the carnivores.

# Efficient Hunters

*Allosaurus* was one of the largest hunters found in the Morrison Formation, reaching up to 12 metres in length.

**L**arge carnivorous dinosaurs, such as *Allosaurus,* developed alongside the enormous herbivorous sauropods. This predator walked on two legs and had short arms with strong claws. It is possible that the carnivores evolved because they were able to take advantage of the large amount of available meat. Small, fast-moving carnivores, such as *Ornitholestes,* fed on animals smaller than themselves, or on leftovers.

**TRACKING**
The hunting scenes that took place here were recorded in footprints! There are many documented footprint trails that show carnivorous dinosaurs tracking sauropods.

**ALLOSAURUS**

Nearly 60 complete *Allosaurus* skeletons have been found in the Morrison Formation!

Skull

Shoulder blade

Ilium or pelvis bone

Tail bones

Humerus or upper arm bone

Femur or thigh bone

Tibia (shin bone), fibula

Radius, ulna (forearm bones)

**STALKING THE PREY**
The herbivore *Camptosaurus,* a close relative of the bird-like dinosaur *Iguanodon,* was prey for *Allosaurus.*

## DIVERSITY OF CARNIVORES

A large number of different theropod dinosaurs have been found in the region – not only skeletons, but also fossilized footprints and droppings. More evidence comes from the teeth marks these predators imprinted in their victims' bones. *Allosaurus*, *Ceratosaurus* and *Torvosaurus* are the best known of these carnivores.

## COMPARISON

The complete skeletons of many theropods have been found in the Morrison Formation. These discoveries have helped palaeontologists to recreate the dinosaurs' body structures with great accuracy. *Torvosaurus* and *Allosaurus* were among the largest, while the smallest were *Stokesosaurus*, *Ornitholestes*, *Coelurus* and *Tanycolagreus*.

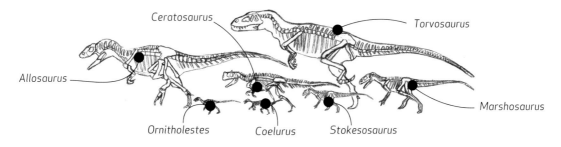

# Stegosaurus

This armoured dinosaur lived in North America 145 million years ago, but its relatives were found on many different continents. *Stegosaurus* ate low-lying plants that were digested in its massive stomach.

The beginning of the Jurassic Period saw the appearance of animals that were two-legged and less than 1 metre in length. These were thyreophorans (meaning 'shield bearers'). These bird-like dinosaurs had body coverings as protection or armour. The best known is *Scutellosaurus*, whose skin was protected by tiny shields of cone shapes. These small creatures were the forerunners of the stegosaurs and the ankylosaurs, which developed larger bodies and thicker, more complex armour.

The stegosaurs had armour along their necks, backs and tails, in the form of large triangular plates and spikes. They were four-legged, with hoof-like claws at the end of their toes. The most ancient stegosaur was *Huayangosaurus*, which was about 3 metres in length, but *Stegosaurus* reached up to 9 metres. At the beginning of the Cretaceous Period, about 130 million years ago, these dinosaurs became extinct, possibly because of competition from new plant-eating species.

GENUS: STEGOSAURUS
CLASSIFICATION: ORNITHISCHIA, THYREOPHORA, STEGOSAURIDAE

**LENGTH** 9 m
**WEIGHT** 5000 kg
**DIET** Herbivorous

**TEMPERATURE REGULATOR**
The plates on *Stegosaurus'* back had a large surface area. It is thought that they helped to control body temperature.

**TEETH**
*Stegosaurus'* teeth were not big enough to chomp food! Instead, food was swallowed and broken down in the digestive system.

**TAIL SPIKES**
Spikes at the end of *Stegosaurus'* tail pointed dangerously to the sides.

**LOCATION**
*Stegosaurus* fossils have been found in rocks in the United States, dating from the end of the Jurassic Period.

Several types of stegosaur fossils have also been found in layers of rocks from the Jurassic Period in Africa, Portugal and China.

# Stegosaurus

Stegosaurs had five toes on their front feet and only three on their back feet. They carried their heads close to the ground, so that they could feed on low-lying plants.

The plates on a stegosaur's back were used in many ways. Firstly as armour for protection, but also for display and recognition so members of the herd could communicate. The large plates had blood vessels near the surface, so they could have been used to control the temperature of the dinosaur's body.

At the end of *Stegosaurus'* tail there were two pairs of long spikes used as a defensive weapon.

The brain cavity in the skull of *Stegosaurus* was very small, but there was a large area of the spinal cord at the hip area. This has led experts to suggest that this dinosaur might have had a 'second brain'.

**LIFE AS A SAUROPOD**
The stegosaurs roamed around with great sauropods, such as *Diplodocus*, *Camarasaurus* and *Apatosaurus*, at the end of the Jurassic Period. They were always in danger of attack from carnivores, such as *Ceratosaurus* and *Allosaurus*.

## PHYLOGENETIC TREE

| PERMIAN | 252 m.a. | TRIASSIC | 201 m.a. | JURASSIC | 145 m.a. | CRETACEOUS | 66 m.a. |
|---------|----------|----------|----------|----------|----------|------------|---------|
| | | | | | | Ankylosaurs | |
| | | Ornithischians | | | | | |
| | | | | Stegosaurs | | | |
| | | | | Ornithopods | | | |

THE DISCOVERER
*Stegosaurus* was first described
and named by Othniel C. Marsh
in 1877. Marsh thought it was
tortoise-like, so he gave it the
name *Stegosaurus,* which means
'roofed reptile', as he thought the
plates were like tiles on a roof.

## STEGOSAURS AROUND THE WORLD

Fossils of other family members of
stegosauria have been found around the
world. They include *Huayangosaurus*
and *Wuerhosaurus* in present-day China,
*Miragaia* in Portugal, and *Kentrosaurus*
in Tanzania.

WUERHOSAURUS

MIRAGAIA

HUAYANGOSAURUS

KENTROSAURUS

**LETHAL TAIL**
*Kentrosaurus* moved its tail from side
to side, striking with its spikes.

**PREY AND PREDATORS**
Some species of stegosaur
defended themselves by lashing
out with their spiked tails.

# Stegosaurus

**BACK PLATES**
The back plates were wide and thin, with an average height and width of approximately 60 cm.

**HIPS**
*Stegosaurus* had features similar to bird-like dinosaurs, with the forward portion of the hip bones pointing downwards and backwards.

**SKELETON**
The back was curved. The front legs were short, and the head was small and carried close to the ground. The tail was strong and held well above the ground.

**SPIKES ON THE TAIL**
*Stegosaurus* used this weapon well, pointing its tail directly towards its enemies.

# Long-necked Dinosaurs

Sauropod dinosaurs were the most gigantic animals ever to walk the Earth. They spread to every corner of the world, and, in Gondwana, they were the most common form of herbivores. Some of them reached a massive 35 metres in length!

**S**auropods first appeared at the end of the Triassic Period, around 200 million years ago. They became the dominant herbivores of the Mesozoic Era and reached their peak during the Jurassic Period.

The word *sauropod* means 'footed lizard'. The sauropods were given this name because of the five short toes on their back legs. These toes were very different from the slim feet of theropods and ornithopods, which were adapted for running. The sauropods were quadrupeds – they walked on four legs. Some could raise themselves up on their back legs to reach a treetop or to defend themselves.

Their heads were very small in relation to the rest of their bodies, and they had simple teeth of various types.

### THE NECK
The sauropods had the longest necks of all dinosaurs and some species had up to 17 neck bones! Their long neck helped them see further and be alert to danger. It also allowed them to reach into the treetops to find leaves and fruit. The bones (vertebrae) had air sacs to help support the long neck.

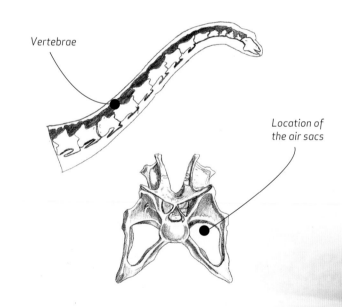

Vertebrae

Location of the air sacs

### CHANGES IN POSTURE
Some sauropods may have been able to balance on their rear legs, supporting themselves with their tails, like a third leg!

## STRENGTHENED NECK

The neck was given extra strength by a ligament (fibrous tissue) that ran along its length. This ligament provided elasticity and support, and helped the dinosaur's movements.

## STRONG BACKS

It is thought that *Diplodocus* could raise itself up on its hind legs when in danger, thanks to the strong muscles running along its back, but this is not known for sure.

## SKULL AND TEETH

The sauropods had a great variety of skull sizes. *Diplodocus* had a long skull with nasal cavities at the top and teeth at the end of the snout. *Camarasaurus* had a short skull with large nasal cavities and teeth along the arch of the mouth.

Eye socket

Nasal cavity

DIPLODOCUS

Nasal cavity

Eye socket

CAMARASAURUS

## WHIP TAIL

Sauropods defended themselves by sudden movements of their whip-like tails.

# Diplodocids and Macronaria

The Late Jurassic Period was the 'golden age' of the sauropods. By that time, the two most important types in this group of herbivores were established: the diplodocids and macronaria.

The diplodocids had wide snouts with teeth at the end, rather like a rake! *Diplodocus* is the best known of all the diplodocids. Other species included *Brachytrachelopan*, which had a much shorter neck, and *Amargasaurus*, which had large spikes on its back.

The macronarian ('large nose') sauropods included the biggest of them all – titanosaurs! These gigantic dinosaurs, including *Puertasaurus*, *Argentinosaurus* and *Futalognkosaurus*, lived in South America during the Cretaceous Period. They were the only sauropods to survive until the end of the Mesozoic Era.

Titanosaurs measured between 30 and 35 metres in length. They all had a stronger skeleton structure than any other dinosaur group. They had shorter tails than diplodocids, which they used to support themselves on their hind legs.

*Dreadnoughtus* was a titanosaur first named in 2014. The fossils were of a young dinosaur, yet it was 26 metres long and weighed 65 tonnes.

**ODD ONE OUT**
*Brachytrachelopan* was an exception among the sauropods because it was small in size and its neck was extremely short. It lived in Patagonia during the Jurassic Period.

**PROTECTION**
Some titanosaurs, such as *Neuquensaurus*, had small plates on their backs. These plates formed a protective covering from predators like *Abelisaurus* and *Austroraptor*.

## BIG AND SMALL

*Brachytrachelopan* was one of the smallest diplodocids, while *Diplodocus* was one of the largest.

DIPLODOCUS

BRACHYTRACHELOPAN

**BODY STRUCTURE**
*Brachytrachelopan* had a curved back and held its head close to the ground.

**LIMITED DIET**
*Brachytrachelopan* fed on low grasses because it could not reach up high.

## BIGGEST GIANT

In the Cretaceous Period, 90 million years ago, *Puertasaurus* lived in Patagonia. This massive dinosaur had a thick neck, which was able to move in every direction.

**LONG NECK**
*Puertasaurus* could have easily reached the tallest treetops.

**HUGE THORAX**
The thorax (between the head and stomach) was so big it could have housed an African elephant.

**LEGS**
The legs were well separated, creating a firm support for the body.

# Brachiosaurs

The larger and more rounded body of *Brachiosaurus* made it stand out from other enormous sauropods. Its front legs were longer than its rear ones, and its back was curved as a result. This feature gave *Brachiosaurus* a rather strange appearance.

The fossil remains of *Brachiosaurus altithorax* were discovered by Elmer Riggs in 1902, in rocks from the Late Jurassic Period in the Morrison Formation. The name *Brachiosaurus* indicates that the front legs were longer than the hind ones. *Altithorax* refers to the high position of the thorax from the ground.

From reconstructions of the skeleton of *Brachiosaurus* we can see that its front legs were more widely separated than those of the diplodocids, and its chest was very wide. It had powerful muscles that supported and balanced its long, strong neck. Its thick, spoon-shaped teeth suggest that *Brachiosaurus* ate hard vegetation which it browsed on from high up in the treetops. Its head may have been up to nine metres above the ground.

It is thought that *Brachiosaurus* lived in herds and may have travelled long distances in search of food, like elephants do today.

GENUS: BRACHIOSAURUS
CLASSIFICATION: SAURISCHIA, SAUROPODA, MACRONARIA

**LENGTH** 26 m
**WEIGHT** 23,000 kg
**DIET** Herbivorous

## NECK
*Brachiosaurus* had to keep its neck out of the reach of predators to avoid being bitten in the throat.

## CLAW TOE
*Brachiosaurus* had only one claw, on the first toe of each front foot. This could have been used for defence.

## LOCATION
*Brachiosaurus* was discovered in the west of the United States, in rocks of the Late Jurassic Period.

*Giraffatitan*, a relative of *Brachiosaurus*, was found in the famous site of Tendaguru, in Tanzania.

# Brachiosaurs

**G**iraffatitan ('titan giraffe') is the best-known brachiosaur, as many fossils of this species have been found in Tanzania, Africa. It is one of the largest dinosaurs we know existed.

The dinosaur was first named by a German palaeontologist in 1914 as a species of brachiosaur. However, in 1991, George Olshevsky placed *Giraffatitan* in its own genus.

Although *Giraffatitan* is a different species to *Brachiosaurus*, it probably had a very similar lifestyle, feeding on vegetation from the treetops. The arrangement of its teeth would have been very efficient at cropping the soft greenery from the Jurassic trees.

**HUMERUS**
The humerus (arm bone) of *Giraffatitan* was thin and measured over 2 m, as long as its thigh bone! These gave the body the appearance of a giraffe.

THE DISCOVERER
Between 1909 and 1912, the German palaeontologist Werner Janensch collected skeletons of *Giraffatitan, Stegosaurus, Kentrosaurus* and the theropod *Elaphrosaurus* in Tanzania.

PHYLOGENETIC TREE

| PERMIAN | 252 m.a. | TRIASSIC | 201 m.a. | JURASSIC | 145 m.a. | CRETACEOUS | 66 m.a. |
|---------|----------|----------|----------|----------|----------|------------|---------|

Theropods

Sauropods

Titanosaurs

**SKULL**

*Giraffatitan* had a skull similar to *Camarasaurus*, but with a wider snout and larger nasal openings.

Nasal cavity

**CHISEL TEETH**
*Giraffatitan* had chisel-like teeth, suitable for a herbivorous diet.

**BACK VERTEBRAE**
*Giraffatitan* had strengthened joints to support the weight of the body.

# Brachiosaurs

**GIRAFFE-LIKE APPEARANCE**
*Brachiosaurus* looked like a giraffe! The forward part of the back was higher than the hip, and the neck pointed upwards.

**SHORT TAIL**
*Brachiosaurus* had a short tail. When walking, it held it above the ground.

**HIP**
The back legs moved with the help of powerful muscles from the upper bone of the hip.

**EATING AT GREAT HEIGHTS**
In the Jurassic Period, araucarias were the tallest trees. They are known as monkey puzzle trees today. They were a source of food for many herbivores. *Brachiosaurus* was able to raise its neck up to 10 m above the ground to reach these trees!

**GIANT STRUCTURE**
The neck was raised in a slight curve shape. The ribcage was enormous and supported by its strong legs.

# Dilophosaurus

*Dilophosaurus* was made famous worldwide by the film *Jurassic Park*. Its most notable feature was the double crest in the upper part of the skull.

A lthough *Jurassic Park* made *Dilophosaurus* famous, it also showed two features the dinosaur definitely did not have in real life – the ability to spit poison and the large fold of skin around the neck which opened rather like an umbrella!

*Dilophosaurus* was a member of a family of ancient two-legged dinosaurs that lived at the end of the Triassic Period and beginning of the Jurassic. Its remains have been found in both North America and Asia. This shows that *Dilophosaurus* was present in large numbers in various places as the Pangea supercontinent was being formed.

Among the ancient relatives of *Dilophosaurus* were *Coelophysis*, *Megapnosaurus*, *Liliensternus* and *Zupaysaurus*. All of them had a long skull, with many teeth. The snout was partly separated from the rest of the head. The neck was thin and very flexible, which meant it could be stretched quickly to allow the dinosaur to catch prey in its mouth.

GENUS: DILOPHOSAURUS
CLASSIFICATION: THEROPODA, COELOPHYSOIDEA

**LENGTH** 6 m
**WEIGHT** 500 kg
**DIET** Carnivorous

**GROUPS**
Hundreds of skeletons of *Coelophysis*, an ancient relative of *Dilophosaurus*, have been found together. This indicates that these dinosaurs lived in groups.

**ARMS**
*Dilophosaurus* had very flexible arms, which it used to grasp and control food.

**LOCATION**
*Dilophosaurus* lived in North America. Its relative *Zupaysaurus* was discovered in Argentina.

*Dilophosaurus sinensis* lived in China. This animal was closely related to the North American *Dilophosaurus*.

# Dilophosaurus

*Dilophosaurus* was one of the largest theropods of the early Jurassic Period, reaching up to 6 metres in length. Its name means 'two lophos (crests) reptile', since its most obvious characteristic was the complex structure of crests on its head. They were only a few millimetres thick, and it is thought that they may have been used for communication and recognition, rather like cockerels use their fleshy 'combs' today.

At the beginning of the Jurassic Period, *Dilophosaurus* was the most dangerous predator, because there were no other large carnivores around at that time.

### OTHER PRIMITIVE DINOSAURS

The theropod *Coelophysis* and the ornithischian *Scutellosaurus* lived together in North America, 190 million years ago. *Scutellosaurus* was a small dinosaur and a distant relative of ankylosaurs and stegosaurs.

COELOPHYSIS

SCUTELLOSAURUS

PHYLOGENETIC TREE

| PERMIAN | | TRIASSIC | | JURASSIC | | CRETACEOUS | |
|---------|---|----------|---|----------|---|------------|---|
| | 252 m.a. | | 201 m.a. | *Dilophosaurus* | 145 m.a. | | 66 m.a. |
| | | Theropods | | | | | |
| | | | | Tetanurans | | | |

**SKELETON**
Skeletons of *Dilophosaurus* have been preserved in excellent condition! They provide us with important data about the body structure of the ancient theropods.

THE DISCOVERER
In 1942, US palaeontologist Samuel P. Welles found an almost complete skeleton of *Dilophosaurus*. Some years later, another one was found with an almost intact skull.

# Dilophosaurus

**LONG TAIL**
*Dilophosaurus* had a large number of bones in its tail. The main function of the tail was to balance the body.

**HANDS**
*Dilophosaurus* had three fingers with claws and a fourth one that was smaller in size. This set the pattern for the structure of the hands of future theropods.

**LEGS**
The legs of *Dilophosaurus* were long and muscular. They had three toes facing forwards and another smaller one pointing to the side. *Dilophosaurus* ran very fast on its hind legs.

**SKULL**
The skull was long, with two crests down the centre of the back. It had wide openings for the nasal cavities and eye sockets.

**CREST**
The head was topped with two delicate crests. They may have been colourful and were probably used to help animals recognize each other.

**NECK**
*Dilophosaurus* had a long, S-shaped neck, similar to some birds today. When the animal was alert or sensed danger, it held its head high to look out over its territory.

# Cretaceous Period

The Cretaceous Period was the longest period in the Mesozoic Era, lasting around 80 million years (145 to 66 million years ago). Large numbers of dinosaurs roamed the Earth in many different sizes and shapes. Enormous pterosaurs flew in the skies alongside the birds, and there were many small insects such as bees and moths.

The Cretaceous Period was a time of warm, humid climate with no ice caps covering the poles. This meant that sea levels were high, with many of the continents covered in warm, shallow waters. There was an explosion of different life forms in this period. Flowering plants appeared, and the dinosaurs continued to develop in many varied forms. These included horned dinosaurs, such as *Triceratops*, small dinosaurs, such as *Velociraptor*, and giant carnivores, such as *Tyrannosaurus rex*.

The Cretaceous Period – and the Mesozoic Era – ended with a massive extinction that saw all the big animals, including the dinosaurs, perish. Scientists believe that this extinction was caused by increased volcanic activity (eruptions), together with the collision of one or more meteorites into the Earth. They think that the dust and ash from these events reduced the amount of sunlight reaching Earth, with catastrophic results for plants and animals.

### PLANTS

Flowering plants appeared around 100 million years ago. They grew alongside the seed-bearing trees (such as conifers), that had dominated the Mesozoic Era up to that time.

### FORESTS

Forests flourished in areas with humid climates and then spread to other parts.

**CRETACEOUS LANDSCAPE**
This period had a relatively warm climate, resulting in high sea levels and shallow inland seas.

**MOUNTAINS**
Mountain ranges such as the Alps in Europe began to form during the Cretaceous Period.

**EARTH'S LAND MASSES**
The positions of the landmasses on planet Earth were similar to their positions today. North America and Europe, Africa and South America separated. As the two American plates moved to the west, they collided with the Pacific Ocean plate, pushing land up at the plate edges to create huge mountain ranges.

**ANIMALS**
Although dinosaurs ruled the world during the Cretaceous Period, many mammals also evolved during this time. *Repenomamus*, found in the north of China, was one of the largest mammals of the Mesozoic Era.

**SUCCESSFUL DINOSAURS**
Dinosaurs existed in huge numbers and varieties during this period, and they spread around the world.

# The Gobi Desert

The Gobi Desert, in the heart of Asia, is famous all over the world for the large quantity of well-preserved dinosaur remains that have been found there. Exploration of this region began early in the 20th century.

**A**n enormous number of vertebrate fossils have been found in the Gobi Desert. The fossils are well preserved, which has led palaeontologists to wonder if a natural disaster may have buried the animals very suddenly.

The first expedition to the Gobi Desert was led by an American explorer, Roy Chapman Andrews, in the 1920s. The first fossilized dinosaur eggs were discovered in Flaming Cliffs, one of the most celebrated sites in the Gobi Desert. The rocks of Flaming Cliffs were formed in an extremely dry climate. Dozens of well-preserved eggs were found here, some with parts of the shell intact!

As the most common species at this site was *Protoceratops*, it was thought that these were *Protoceratops* eggs. A different dinosaur found buried on top of a clutch of eggs was assumed to be a predator. This animal was named *Oviraptor*, which means 'egg thief'. However, new research in the 1980s proved that the eggs belonged to *Oviraptor* and not *Protoceratops*!

**MARKS FROM THE PAST**
Many dinosaur footprints have been found in Gobi Desert rocks. One of them is thought to be a footprint of *Protoceratops*.

**A GOBI EXPLORER**
Roy Chapman Andrews led several expeditions to the Gobi Desert, organized and funded by the American Museum of Natural History in New York, USA.

**FLAMING CLIFFS**
Dozens of fossilized egg remains were found in this location. Although *Protoceratops* may have built their raised nests here, it is now thought that most of the eggs found at Flaming Cliffs belonged to *Oviraptor*.

# Origin of Birds

The origin of birds has been much debated. Many palaeontologists today believe that birds are related to flesh-eating, two-legged dinosaurs. The two groups have similarities in bones, eggs and behaviour. The discovery of spectacular fossils in China prove that many dinosaurs had feathers. The most detailed studies point to maniraptorans (a group that includes oviraptors) being the direct ancestors of birds.

## REPTILIAN INHERITANCE

Maniraptors and theropods have a lot of physical similarities to birds, which can be seen on the skeleton.

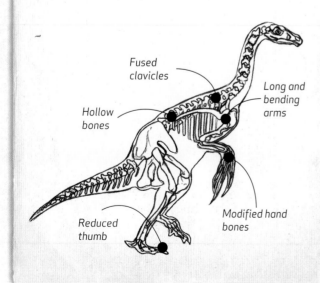

Fused clavicles

Long and bending arms

Hollow bones

Reduced thumb

Modified hand bones

### INCUBATING
Some oviraptorid skeletons have been found on top of nests. This proved that dinosaurs sat on their eggs to provide warmth and to help them hatch.

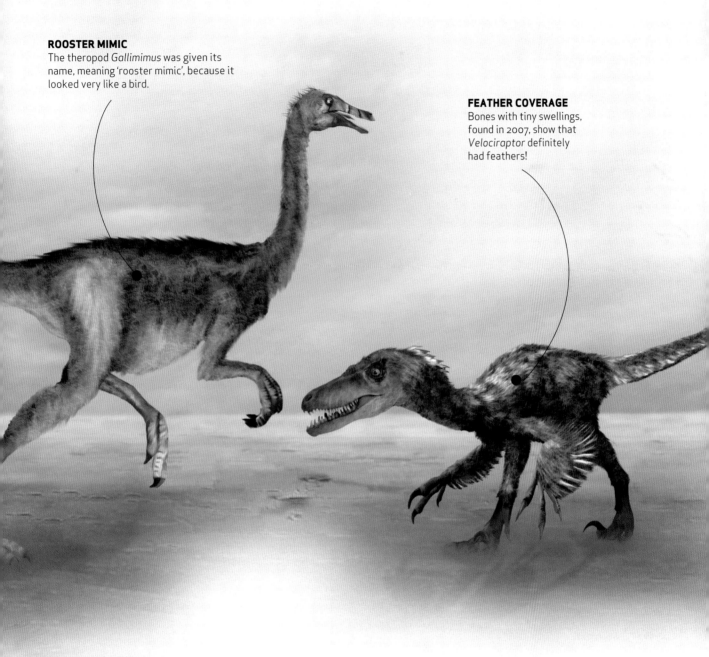

**ROOSTER MIMIC**
The theropod *Gallimimus* was given its name, meaning 'rooster mimic', because it looked very like a bird.

**FEATHER COVERAGE**
Bones with tiny swellings, found in 2007, show that *Velociraptor* definitely had feathers!

**FEATHER EVOLUTION**

In the beginning, the purpose of feathers was to maintain body heat. Later on, they became useful for flying.

Growing pimple from inside a pod

*Beipiaosaurus*

Strands appear in the pimple

*Sinosauropteryx*

Branched outgrowths develop

*Sinornithosaurus*

Hooks appear in the outgrowths

*Caudipteryx*

Feathers are similar to those of today

*Archaeopteryx*

# Spinosaurus

An extraordinary predator that hunted on land and in water, *Spinosaurus* was one of the most gigantic theropods ever to walk on Earth.

Some palaeontologists believe that *Spinosaurus* reached up to 18 metres in length and around 8 tonnes in weight, leaving both *Tyrannosaurus rex* and *Giganotosaurus* behind! Discoveries made in countries such as Niger, Morocco, Britain and Brazil have provided us with information about the structure and lifestyle of these amazing dinosaurs. Other notable features include a massive skull, 1.75 metres long, and rows of spines on the back, which measured up to 1.65 metres!

The spinosaurids were a special type of theropod, with long snouts and cone-shaped teeth like those of crocodiles. The digested remains of fish scales and bones, as well as the remains of a young *Iguanodon*, have been found inside the ribs of fossils of the spinosaurid *Baryonyx*. In Brazil, the mark of a *Spinosaurus* tooth was discovered on a neck bone of a pterosaur, a flying reptile. From this and other evidence, it's clear that the spinosaurid's diet included fish, young herbivorous dinosaurs and flying reptiles.

Recent studies reveal that *Spinosaurus aegypticus* was a semi-aquatic dinosaur, with short, powerful hind legs adapted for paddling in water.

GENUS: SPINOSAURUS
CLASSIFICATION: THEROPODA, TETANURAE, SPINOSAURIDAE

**LENGTH** 12.5–18 m
**WEIGHT** 5000–9000 kg
**DIET** Carnivorous

**LEGS**
They were strong enough to support the body weight, which was increased by the extra weight of its spiny back.

**TEETH**
There were around 40 teeth in its mouth, with the largest at the very tip of the snout.

**HANDS**
The inner finger had a strong and curved claw. It was used as a deadly weapon.

**LOCATION**
Skulls of *Irritator* and *Oxalaia*, one of the largest spinosaurids, were discovered in Brazil.

*Baryonyx* came from England, and the large spinosaurids *Suchomimus* and *Spinosaurus* from Africa.

# Spinosaurus

*Spinosaurus* was well suited to catching fish. Its skull has similarities to that of crocodiles, at the edges of the mouth and in the shape of the teeth. Like crocodiles, *Spinosaurus* may have had pressure sensors at the tip of the snout that helped it to detect prey moving in water. This meant that it could strike at fish without being able to see them!

The huge spines running along its back have confused palaeontologists. Could they have formed a kind of 'sail'? A sail would have helped to control body temperature by taking in heat when the animal was facing the sun. However, recent studies suggest that the spines on the back supported a large hump of fat, similar to those on camels or bison. This hump would have stored energy to allow the dinosaur to survive during times when there was little food or water.

*Spinosaurus* shared the environment with other carnivores, such as *Carcharodontosaurus*. But it seems that they did not compete for food resources. *Spinosaurus* fed mainly on fish, while *Carcharodontosaurus* fed on land-based, herbivorous dinosaurs.

**THE DISCOVERER**
In 1912, the German palaeontologist Ernst Stromer found the first remains of *Spinosaurus* in Egypt. Unfortunately, this skeleton was destroyed in a bombing raid during the Second World War.

## PHYLOGENETIC TREE

| PERMIAN | 252 m.a. | TRIASSIC | 201 m.a. | JURASSIC | 145 m.a. | CRETACEOUS | 66 m.a. |
|---------|----------|----------|----------|----------|----------|------------|---------|
| | | | | | | Spinosaurids | |
| | | | | Tetanurans | | | |
| Theropods | | | | | | | |
| | | | | | | Coelurosaurs | |

## GOOD SWIMMER?

To be able to find and catch its prey effectively, *Spinosaurus* was probably a good swimmer.

*Flapping tail*

**SKELETON**

The skeleton shows that *Spinosaurus* was a biped, but they may have crouched or rested on all four limbs.

# Spinosaurus

**LONG HEAD**
Spinosaurus' head had a narrow snout with a hook-like tip and many sharp, pointed teeth.

**TEETH**
The teeth of Spinosaurus were cone-shaped and less curved than in other theropods. They are similar to the teeth of modern-day crocodiles.

**ARMS**
Spinosaurus had long, strong arms, very different from those of the tyrannosaurids. The fingers on the hands had highly developed claws.

**SAIL**
The spines which supported the sail were massive – over 10 times longer than the diameter of the vertebrae that they grew from.

# Suchomimus

*Suchomimus* was a fish-eating dinosaur that spent most of its time in or near water. It also captured other dinosaurs and pterosaurs. This behaviour and some of its physical features make it similar to present-day crocodiles.

This dinosaur's fossils were found in rocks of the Late Cretaceous in Niger, Africa. The specimen was between 11 and 12 metres in length, which makes it one of the largest known theropods.

The structure of *Suchomimus* is similar to other dinosaurs of that period, including *Irritator* and *Oxalaia*, both of which were found in Brazil in South America. This is not surprising as, 120 million years ago, Africa was closer to South America than it is today. This meant that dinosaurs, crocodiles and freshwater fish could have moved from one continent to another.

*Suchomimus* had around 100 cone-shaped teeth, which had crests that locked firmly and allowed the dinosaur to grip slippery fish. The head was long and carried low, with nasal cavities higher than the tip of the snout to keep them above water when the snout was beneath the surface.

GENUS: SUCHOMIMUS
CLASSIFICATION: THEROPODA,
TETANURAE, SPINOSAURIDAE

**LENGTH** 12 m
**WEIGHT** 5000 kg
**DIET** Carnivorous

**BREATHING HOLES**
The nasal openings were on top of the head, allowing the animal to breathe while its snout was under the water.

**ARMS**
*Suchomimus* had very strong arms that were good for hunting and fishing.

**LOCATION**
The remains of two spinosaurids from the Cretaceous Period were found in Brazil: *Irritator* and the massive *Oxalaia*.

*Suchomimus* was found in Niger, Africa, and its most evolved relative, *Spinosaurus*, in Egypt.

**CLAWS**
The claws were like those of *Baryonyx*, an older relative of *Suchomimus*.

# Suchomimus

*Suchomimus* had neural spines along its back, but they were lower than in *Spinosaurus*. It is thought that these carnivorous dinosaurs carried a hump of energy-storing fat on their backs. Evidence indicates that their main source of food was fish but, like *Spinosaurus*, *Suchomimus* would catch and eat other animals if necessary.

An interesting adaptation of *Suchomimus* was the huge sickle-curved claw on its thumb. All the arm bones were very strong, indicating that the limbs were useful for powerful movement and hunting.

THE DISCOVERER
*Suchomimus* was found by Paul Sereno of the University of Chicago in the United States, during a scientific expedition to the Sahara in 1997.

## PHYLOGENETIC TREE

| PERMIAN | 252 m.a. | TRIASSIC | 201 m.a. | JURASSIC | 145 m.a. | CRETACEOUS | 66 m.a. |
|---------|----------|----------|----------|----------|----------|------------|---------|
| | | | | | | Spinosaurids | |
| | | | | Tetanurans | | Carnosaurs | |
| | | Theropods | | | | Coelurosaurs | |

## DIET

The structure of *Suchomimus'* jaws, together with the shape of its teeth and the fossilized contents of its stomach, suggests that its main prey was fish. It may have eaten fish like this *Lepidotes*.

## CROCODILE MIMIC

*Suchomimus* got its name from its skull, which is very like that of a crocodile, with a long, low snout.

## ARMS

*Suchomimus* had long arms, with large, curved claws on the hands.

# Suchomimus

**HUMP**
The spinal bones on the back supported a hump similar to a camel's. They were shorter than those of *Spinosaurus*, the gigantic descendant of *Suchomimus*.

**STRONG LEGS**
*Suchomimus* used its strong legs for plunging into rivers to catch fish, and probably also for swimming.

**SKULL**
The skull of *Suchomimus* was over 1 m in length.

**SNOUT**
*Suchomimus* had a long, narrow snout. Its teeth were arranged in a similar way to those of modern-day gharials (a type of crocodile).

**SKELETON**
The first discovery of a complete skeleton of *Suchomimus* was of a young animal that was not fully developed. When fully grown, it would have been similar in size to a *Tyrannosaurus*.

# Iguanodon

Large numbers of *Iguanodon* fossils have been found in many different parts of the world. From this evidence, we know that they formed groups, roaming together in search of food.

*guanodon*, meaning 'iguana tooth', was a dinosaur that lived in Europe in the Middle Cretaceous Period, some 125 million years ago. It was a large, strong herbivore that moved on either two or four legs, resting its hoof-like fingers on the ground.

Adult animals measured around 10 metres in length, although some could reach up to 13 metres. The skull was tall, with a narrow snout ending in a toothless beak.

Although first found in England in 1822, the most extraordinary discovery of *Iguanodon* remains came from a coal mine at Bernissart in Belgium, in 1878. Bones from 38 animals were gathered from this mine, allowing the Belgian palaeontologist Louis Dollo to assemble several skeletons and learn more about these spectacular dinosaurs.

GENUS: IGUANODON
CLASSIFICATION: ORNITHISCHIA, ORNITHOPODA, IGUANODONTIA

**LENGTH** 10 m
**WEIGHT** 5000 kg
**DIET** Herbivorous

**CHEWING**
The structure of the beak, together with the movement of its jaw, helped *Iguanodon* to grind up its food.

**LOCATION**
Remains of *Iguanodon* have been found in Europe, and the unusual iguanodont *Ouranosaurus* was discovered in Africa.

# Iguanodon

The iguanodonts are grouped together within the Ornithopoda category. The name *Ornithopoda*, meaning 'bird foot', comes from the fact that many dinosaurs in this group had three fingers, similar to those of birds.

Ornithopod fossils have been found worldwide – even in Antarctica! These animals first appeared in the Middle Jurassic Period, reaching their maximum numbers in the Cretaceous Period.

There were two main ancestries: the small, light hypsilophodonts and the more developed, large and heavy iguanodonts. The hypsilophodonts measured less than 2 metres long on average. They were two-legged and could run fast when attacked. Their tails were long, with hardened connecting tissues to help them balance while running.

The iguanodonts included *Iguanodon bernissartensis* as well as its close cousins *Dryosaurus*, *Camptosaurus* and *Talenkauen*.

Scientists now believe that *Iguanodon atherfieldensis* should be called *Mantellisaurus*, after Gideon Mantell, who discovered it.

**OURANOSAURUS**

This extraordinary-looking iguanodont lived in Africa in the Early Cretaceous Period. It had a large hump of fat on its back supported by neural spines.

*Tall neural spines on back*

*Neural spines on tail*

THE DISCOVERER
*Iguanodon* was only the second dinosaur to be given a scientific name (after *Megalosaurus*). It was discovered and named by the British scientist Gideon Mantell in the 1820s.

## PHYLOGENETIC TREE

| PERMIAN | | TRIASSIC | | JURASSIC | | CRETACEOUS | |
|---|---|---|---|---|---|---|---|
| | 252 m.a. | | 201 m.a. | | 145 m.a. | | 66 m.a. |

Ornithopods

Iguanodonts

Ornithischians

Marginocephalians

Ceratopsians

**SKELETON**
The hind legs were very strong, to carry the whole weight of *Iguanodon* when it stood on two legs.

**SPIKED THUMB**
The thumb of *Iguanodon* formed a big spike. When the fossil remains of *Iguanodon* were first assembled, the thumb spike was thought to have been a horn on its nose!

# Iguanodon

**IGUANA TEETH**
*Iguanodon's* teeth were arranged in long rows at the sides of the mouth. Each one of them was similar to a modern iguana's tooth, but much larger.

**HANDS**
The hands were strong and rigid. The big spike on the thumb was used for defence, while the middle fingers supported the body weight. The outer finger was able to turn back against the other fingers, rather like a human thumb.

**HIP**
The front portion of the hip bones was directed backwards. This position helped in the development of the digestive system by allowing more space for a large stomach and, therefore, more efficient digestion.

**LEGS**
*Iguanodon* mainly moved on all four limbs, although it could also stand on two legs if it needed to reach higher vegetation or fight off rivals and predators.

# Carnivores

*Theropod* means 'beast feet' and indicates that dinosaurs in this group had pointed claws at their toes. Theropods were carnivores, well suited to running and hunting efficiently.

Carnivorous dinosaurs are grouped within Theropoda, one of the main ancestries. Together with the herbivorous sauropodomorphs, Theropoda form the large group of saurischian dinosaurs. The earliest theropods appeared during the Late Triassic Period, 230 million years ago. They already had features that included sharp and curved teeth, loose arms with cutting claws, hips adapted for fast movement and long tails to help the animals balance themselves.

The oldest theropods, *Herrerasaurus* and *Eoraptor*, were discovered in Argentina. *Eoraptor* was around 1 metre in length, but *Herrerasaurus* was a bigger predator. In North America, more advanced theropods, such as *Coelophysis* and *Dilophosaurus,* emerged from these early forms. At the end of the Jurassic Period, the first large theropods appeared – *Allosaurus,* for example, which reached up to 12 metres in length. Varied forms appeared during the Cretaceous Period, from the very large, such as *Giganotosaurus,* to the pigeon-sized *Ligabueino*.

Tetanuran theropods included a wide range of forms, from gigantic predators to small, insect-eating animals. Their evolution is still continuing today, as birds are examples of this group.

THEROPOD LEG
Palaeontologist Othniel C. Marsh invented the term *Theropoda.* He discovered fossils of *Allosaurus* (whose leg appears in this photo) and *Ceratosaurus,* both from the Jurassic Period.

**BIG HUNTERS**
*Allosaurus* lived at the end of the Jurassic Period, around 146 million years ago. It fed on lizard-hipped and bird-hipped dinosaurs such as *Dryosaurus*.

## SHORT AND LONG

*Alvarezsaurus* had very short arms that hardly extended from its body. It used them to dig into termite mounds in search of food. *Epidendrosaurus*, however, had very long fingers, which it used to catch insects from the bark of trees.

*Alvarezsaurus*

*Epidendrosaurus*

## THEROPOD HIP

Theropod hip bones had large areas where big leg muscles were attached. This allowed them to run quickly in order to chase their prey.

# Ceratosaurs

During the Jurassic Period, the ceratosaurs ('horned reptiles') and the tetanurans ('stiff tails') were the two main ancestries of theropod dinosaurs. *Ceratosaurus* and *Carnotaurus*, from the Cretaceous Period, are two examples of ceratosaurs.

During the Cretaceous Period, the abelisaurs were the ceratosaurs that dominated Gondwana. *Carnotaurus* was the grandest of them all. It got its name from its flesh-eating habits and its horns, which were similar to those of a bull. Its skeleton was found in rocks in South America, but close relatives have also been found in India, Africa and Madagascar. It had tiny forelimbs that were practically useless, but hind legs that were slender, sleek and well adapted for running. The skull was short and broad and attached to a very strong, wide neck. *Carnotaurus* was around nine metres long and weighed over a tonne.

THE DISCOVERER
The only skeleton of *Carnotaurus* was found in 1984 by an Argentinian palaeontologist called José Bonaparte. It was embedded in a very hard kind of rock, so it was very difficult to dig out! Bonaparte described this new species in 1985 as *Carnotaurus sastrei*.

**SKIN**
*Carnotaurus'* skin was covered with scale-like bumps and wrinkles, probably for protection from attack.

**MULTIPURPOSE FEET**
Theropod feet were adapted to support the weight of the dinosaur, to provide power for jumping and speed for running. They had three toes and sharp, pointed claws.

**THEROPOD DIVERSITY**
The separation of Laurasia and Gondwana in the Cretaceous Period gave rise to different theropod forms in different regions: tyrannosaurs and ornithomimids in the north; carcharadontosaurs, abelisaurs and unenlagids in the south.

*Coelurus* was 2.4 m long.

*Gallimimus* was 6 m long.

**HORNS**
*Carnotaurus* had strong outgrowths that pointed outwards, similar to those of a bull.

**JAWS**
*Carnotaurus* had many sharp teeth.

*Ekrixinatosaurus* was a relative of *Carnotaurus* and was 11 m long.

*Daspletosaurus* was part of the tyrannosaurid family and was 9 m long.

*Tyrannotitan* was a relative of *Giganotosaurus* and was 12.2 m long.

# Giganotosaurus

As its name suggests, *Giganotosaurus* was a gigantic dinosaur, one of the biggest carnivorous dinosaurs ever to have existed! It lived in South America around 90 million years ago.

This 'giant southern reptile' was an enormous predator. It was 13.5 metres long, and its skull measured 1.8 metres! It had a large mouth with teeth so sharp that one bite easily slashed through the flesh and muscles of its prey.

*Giganotosaurus* had extremely strong bones, particularly in its hind legs, which were thicker and wider than those of an African elephant. Its huge body weight and the size of its legs indicate that this animal had a slow and heavy walk, so it could not have run to hunt its prey. However, as it preyed upon titanosaurs, who couldn't run fast either, this was not a disadvantage.

*Giganotosaurus* belongs to a group of huge theropod dinosaurs known as the carcharodontosaurids, which included perhaps the largest land predators ever known. The group includes *Carcharodontosaurus* itself, *Tyrannotitan* and *Mapusaurus*.

GENUS: GIGANOTOSAURUS
CLASSIFICATION: THEROPODA, TETANURAE, CARNOSAURIA

**LENGTH** 13.5 m
**WEIGHT** 8000 kg
**DIET** Carnivorous

**HUGE SKULL**
The skull of *Giganotosaurus* was one of the largest among the theropods. Compared with the rest of the body, the head was supersized.

**LOCATION**
*Giganotosaurus* and its relatives *Tyrannotitan* and *Mapusaurus* have been found in Cretaceous Period rocks in Patagonia, Argentina.

*Carcharodontosaurus* was found in Egypt, and *Concavenator*, a smaller relative, was found in Spain.

# Giganotosaurus

*Concavenator*, the oldest known carcharodontosaur, was found in Spain in rocks that were 130 million years old. This specimen was about 6 metres long, but some of its later relatives were bigger.

The name *Carcharodontosaurus* means 'shark-toothed reptile', because these dinosaurs had very sharp teeth, similar to those of a shark. They had around 70 teeth to allow them to cut through meat, although the teeth were probably not strong enough to crunch bones.

*Giganotosaurus* and the carcharodontosaurs were some of the main carnivores populating Gondwana between 125 and 90 million years ago. But their numbers decreased, leading to their complete disappearance several million years before the massive extinction at the end of the Cretaceous Period. The disappearance of the carcharodontosaurs, 90 million years ago, is still a mystery!

**TEETH**
*Giganotosaurus* had short, thin teeth, suitable for slicing through flesh!

THE DISCOVERER
An amateur fossil hunter called Rubén Carolini discovered *Giganotosaurus carolinii* in 1993. The fossil was described by the Argentinian palaeontologists Rodolfo Coria and Leonardo Salgado, who named it after its discoverer.

## PHYLOGENETIC TREE

| PERMIAN | 252 m.a. | TRIASSIC | 201 m.a. | JURASSIC | 145 m.a. | CRETACEOUS | 66 m.a. |
|---------|----------|----------|----------|----------|----------|------------|---------|
| | | | | | | Carnosaurs | |
| | | Theropods | | | | Coelurosaurs | |

**SMELL**
It is believed that *Giganotosaurus'* sense of smell was more developed than its sight, as smell was very helpful for detecting its prey.

**THE LARGEST PREDATORS**

*Giganotosaurus* was bigger and heavier than *Tyrannosaurus rex*. But *Spinosaurus*, found in Africa, was the largest land predator, reaching up to 18 m in length!

**PREY**
*Giganotosaurus* could knock down large herbivorous dinosaurs, such as titanosaurs.

**BALANCING ACT**
The tail balanced the body when the animal moved.

# Giganotosaurus

**ARMS**
It is believed that *Giganotosaurus* had short but strong arms, with three clawed fingers.

**SKULL**
To reduce the weight of *Giganotosaurus'* huge skull, there were large cavities near its eyes.

**HEAVY LEGS**
*Giganotosaurus* walked on its huge, powerful back legs, which were supported by the central toes of its feet.

**POWERFUL TAIL**
The tail had many bones and powerful muscles in order to balance the body. This allowed *Giganotosaurus* to turn its body quickly and attack suddenly.

# Deinonychus

**FEATHERS**
The tip of the tail was covered with feathers, but it is not known whether it had the wide range of feathers that have been found in *Microraptor* and *Caudipteryx*.

*Deinonychus* relied on its lethal, sickle-shaped claws for attack and defence. Its name actually means 'terrible claw'!

In 1964, the American palaeontologist John Ostrom and his team discovered around 1000 *Deinonychus* bones at a site in the west of the United States. The specimens included many well-preserved parts, including skulls. Ostrom also found a large number of eggshells underneath adult bones. This indicated that *Deinonychus* provided warmth for its eggs by sitting on them, in the same way that present-day birds hatch their eggs.

*Deinonychus* lived in hot, humid forests with other carnivores, including the large theropod *Acrocanthosaurus*, the ankylosaur *Sauropelta*, the ornithopod *Tenontosaurus* and the enormous sauropod *Sauroposeidon*. *Deinonychus* is one of the best-known members of the dromaeosauridae family, which also includes dinosaurs such as *Microraptor*, *Unenlagia* and *Utahraptor*.

GENUS: DEINONYCHUS
CLASSIFICATION: THEROPODA, COELUROSAURIA, DEINONYCHOSAURIA

**LENGTH** 3.5 m
**WEIGHT** 80 kg
**DIET** Carnivorous

### *LINHERAPTOR* SKELETON
This almost complete skeleton of *Linheraptor*, a close relative of *Deinonychus*, was found in Mongolia.

### HUNTER'S ARMS
*Deinonychus'* arms folded at the sides of the body but could quickly stretch out to capture prey.

### LOCATION
In the United States, *Deinonychus* fossils have been found in rocks that are 110 million years old.

In Asia, many deinonychosaurs, including *Microraptor*, *Velociraptor* and *Linheraptor*, have been found.

# Deinonychus

The dromaeosaurids appeared in the middle of the Jurassic Period and disappeared at the end of the Cretaceous Period. *Velociraptor* was the first to be discovered by palaeontologists in 1923, in the Gobi Desert, Mongolia. Since then, feathered dinosaurs such as *Sinornithosaurus millenii* have been found in other places, particularly in China.

The dromaeosaurids are thought to be closely related to the troodontids, theropods that also had a sickle-shaped claw on each foot. Because of this strange weapon that they had in common, dromaeosaurids and troodontids are grouped together as *deinonychosaurs*, which means 'fearsome claw reptiles'.

It was Ostrom who first drew attention to the noticeable similarities between *Deinonychus* and *Archaeopteryx*, the oldest known bird. He changed the way palaeontologists thought about dinosaurs, suggesting that they had far more in common with big, flightless birds (such as ostriches) than with reptiles.

**BLADE TEETH**
*Deinonychus* had powerful jaws, with around 70 curved, blade-like teeth.

THE DISCOVERER
The North American palaeontologist John Ostrom, pictured with a reconstructed skeleton of *Deinonychus*. His theories about the links between dinosaurs and birds caused great controversy amongst palaeontologists, and sparked new research into the evolution of birds.

*PHYLOGENETIC TREE*

| PERMIAN | 252 m.a. | TRIASSIC | 201 m.a. | JURASSIC | 145 m.a. | CRETACEOUS | 66 m.a. |
|---------|----------|----------|----------|----------|----------|------------|---------|
| | | | | | | | Dromaeosaurids |
| | | | | Maniraptors | | Birds | |
| | | Coelurosaurs | | | | Oviraptorosaurs | |

**SKELETON**
The thorax was short and upright, similar to birds. The neck curved upwards, holding the head in a high position.

**CLAWED FEET**
The claw on the second toe was up to 13 cm long and very sharp!

# Deinonychus

**SKULL**
*Deinonychus* had strong jaws, with many small, sharp teeth. The snout was narrow, and its bite was very powerful.

**TAIL**
The bones at the tip of the tail were connected by long, hardened tissues, making it very strong. This helped *Deinonychus* to maintain its balance.

**HANDS**
*Deinonychus* had large hands with three long fingers ending in curved claws. These were helpful for grasping and tearing prey.

**SHARP VISION**
The structure of the bones in the skull allowed both eyes to face forwards, which gave *Deinonychus* good 3D vision.

**HUNTING IN PACKS**
Several skeletons of *Deinonychus* and
the ornithopod *Tenontosaurus* were
found together in the United States. This
suggests that they hunted in groups or
gathered together to feed.

# Triceratops

*Triceratops horridus* ('three-horned face') lived in North America during the last 3 million years of the Mesozoic Era.

Triceratops was described for the first time in 1889, and since then hundreds of examples have been found, including specimens of both young and mature animals. This herbivore had a huge skull, around 2.5 metres long, and reached 9 metres in length and 3 metres in height. It is believed that the largest animals may have weighed 11 tonnes! *Triceratops* was a four-legged dinosaur that could not raise itself up on its hind legs. It fed on low, tough plants that it cut with its powerful beak. The front limbs had three fingers, while the back legs had four toes, all of them with rounded hooves.

*Triceratops* had a short horn above the nostrils and two long horns above its eyes. Underneath, the long horns were part of the bone structure of the skull, but the bone was covered by the horn material. Just like present-day bulls, buffaloes and antelopes, the horns regrew if they wore out or broke off.

GENUS: TRICERATOPS
CLASSIFICATION: ORNITHISCHIA,
MARGINOCEPHALIA, CERATOPSIA

**LENGTH** 9 m
**WEIGHT** 12,000 kg
**DIET** Herbivorous

**NECK PLATE**
The rear part of the skull pointed backwards, to form a protective neck covering.

**BEAK JAWS**
*Triceratops* had powerful jaws that were tipped with a pointed beak.

**LOCATION**
*Triceratops* has been found in North America. It is unknown in other parts of the world.

Distant relatives of *Triceratops* have been found in Asia, most of them without horns.

# Triceratops

Like all ceratopsians, *Triceratops* had a large outgrowth of bones at the back of the skull which protected the soft neck area. Research suggests that it used its horns as defensive weapons against predators, such as *Tyrannosaurus rex*. However, in dinosaurs such as *Styracosaurus* the horns were only a few centimetres thick, so they wouldn't have been strong enough for this.

Skulls have been found of both young and adult *Triceratops*. The young animals had already developed horns and neck frills, but as each *Triceratops* grew older, the horns grew in length and thickness. The bony neck plate grew backwards and became thinner.

Both the horns and the neck plates may have helped *Triceratops* parents to recognize their offspring, as each dinosaur would have had small differences in the size and shape of their horns and neck frills. They may also have been used to show dominance among other *Triceratops*, and to help find a mate.

## HORN EVOLUTION

Ceratopsians evolved from having very small horns and neck frills, like *Leptoceratops*, into larger and more varied forms, such as *Pentasaurus*.

*Leptoceratops* had a short snout.

*Eoceratops* had small horns.

*Anchiceratops* had a short neck frill but longer horns and snout.

*Triceratops* grew longer horns, neck frill and snout.

*Pentasaurus* had longer horns again.

## PHYLOGENETIC TREE

| PERMIAN | 252 m.a. | TRIASSIC | 201 m.a. | JURASSIC | 145 m.a. | CRETACEOUS | 66 m.a. |
|---------|----------|----------|----------|----------|----------|------------|---------|

Ceratopsians

Marginocephalians

Ornithischians

**SKELETON**
You can see the neck plate is part of the skull in this reconstruction of the skeleton of *Triceratops horridus*.

**POSTURE**
Palaeontologists originally thought that *Triceratops'* front legs pointed in an outward direction, similar to present-day reptiles, Today, we know that they had a straighter posture, as shown in the lower picture.

# Triceratops

**THREE-HORNED FACE**
The name *Triceratops* means 'three-horned face'. As well as these horns, *Triceratops* had many small spikes along the edge of its neck frill.

**TEETH**
*Triceratops'* teeth were arranged in groups, called batteries. The largest animals could have had up to 800!

**FEET**
The feet ended in rounded hooves with four short toes.

**TAIL**
The tail was short. It was not needed to balance the body, as it did for *Triceratops'* two-footed ancestors.

**FRONT LEGS**
The powerful front legs supported the weight at the front of the body and provided extra strength when attacking enemies.

# Warm- or Cold-blooded?

Scientists share the view that dinosaurs had more advanced behaviour, skills and adaptations than present-day reptiles. Due to their many similarities with birds, today it is thought that instead of being cold-blooded many dinosaurs were warm-blooded.

DINOSAUR HERESIES
Robert Bakker studied with John Ostrom in the 1960s and strongly supported the view that dinosaurs were warm-blooded animals. His book *The Dinosaur Heresies* presented these new ideas to the general public and caused great controversy when it was published in 1986.

For a long time, palaeontologists believed dinosaurs were slow-moving, cold-blooded animals. But new research carried out by John Ostrom challenged these views.

Alongside Ostrom, American palaeontologist Robert Bakker supported the view that dinosaurs were warm-blooded animals, similar to birds and mammals. Bakker argued that the position of dinosaurs' legs straight underneath their bodies, and their ability to move fast with long steps, provided evidence to support this. He showed that they had hair and feathers, similar to warm-blooded birds and mammals, which would have helped to preserve heat in the body. This further supported the idea that many dinosaurs were warm-blooded animals.

## COLD OR WARM

In cold-blooded animals, such as toads, the body temperature varies according to the surrounding air temperature. In warm-blooded animals, such as hamsters, body temperature remains roughly constant and is controlled internally by the body.

*Toad*

*Hamster*

**FEATHER COVERINGS**
Many dinosaurs, including *Psittacosaurus*, were covered in feathers.

**BEAK**
*Psittacosaurus* had a powerful beak on its upper jaw.

**FAST RUNNER**
*Psittacosaurus* could walk on two or four legs. It may have been a fast runner, which would have helped this dinosaur escape predators.

# Diet and Environment

Cold-blooded carnivores only need to consume small amounts of food. However, warm-blooded predators, such as lions, need a larger amount of food for energy and to maintain body temperature.

Some palaeontologists doubted whether herbivorous dinosaurs could be warm-blooded. They thought that slow-growing Mesozoic plants, such as conifers, cycads, ginkgos and ferns, would not have been enough to sustain these dinosaurs. However, in various experiments, ginkgos were grown in atmospheric conditions identical to the climate of the Mesozoic Era. It was found that the ginkgos grew better and had far more nutrients (substances needed for growth) than they do in today's conditions! Therefore, it's likely that conditions in the time of the dinosaurs would have allowed even warm-blooded herbivores to get enough food.

## FIRST DISCOVERIES

The first sign that there was such a thing as polar dinosaurs came in 1960, when dinosaur footprints were found at Spitsbergen, an island between the coast of Norway and the North Pole.

## POLAR DINOSAURS

In 2009, fossil hunters in north-eastern Russia discovered the remains of duck-billed dinosaurs, teeth belonging to relatives of *Triceratops* and even tyrannosaurid teeth! This area would have been inside the Arctic circle when the dinosaurs were alive, with temperatures as low as 10 degrees Celsius.

## LIVING FOSSILS

Ginkgos are non-flowering plants that date back around 270 million years. Ginkgo fossils have been found in many parts of the world. These plants still grow today.

**DARKNESS**
Polar dinosaurs may have had to
endure prolonged darkness for
up to six months each winter.

**FEATHERS**
Feathers may have helped
polar dinosaurs to retain
body heat in order to
survive in cold climates.

# Argentinosaurus

*Argentinosaurus* is the largest dinosaur we know existed. The study of this giant has helped us to learn more about enormous plant-eating sauropods.

**A**rgentinosaurus *huinculensis* was named after the Huincul Formation in south-west Argentina, where palaeontologists found its fossil in 1993. Its scientific name means 'Argentinean lizard'. Only parts of the skeleton were recovered, including some vertebrae, ribs, a shin bone and thigh bone.

When it was first discovered, *Argentinosaurus* attracted international attention because of its size. Sauropods of similar sizes include *Paralititan, Supersaurus, Seismosaurus, Sauroposeidon, Alamosaurus* and *Puertasaurus*.

In 2014, a possible *Argentinosaurus* fossil was discovered near Trelew, Argentina. At 40 metres long and weighing 77 tonnes, this dinosaur could be the largest ever discovered!

## BONES

Like most dinosaurs of such a size, *Argentinosaurus* had around 230 bones in its skeleton. But, despite its great length, the neck contained only 13 vertebrae.

## BIG BACKBONE

One of *Argentinosaurus*'s vertebrae was 1.6 m high and 1.3 m wide! This gives some idea of the enormous size of this dinosaur.

GENUS: ARGENTINOSAURUS
CLASSIFICATION: SAURISCHIA,
SAUROPODA, TITANOSAURIA

**LENGTH** 30 m
**WEIGHT** 73,000 kg
**DIET** Herbivorous

## LOCATION

*Argentinosaurus* was found near to Plaza Huincul, in the south-west of Argentina.

Titanosaurs like *Argentinosaurus* lived during the Cretaceous Period in South America, North America, Africa, Asia and Europe.

# Argentinosaurus

The reason for the giant size of *Argentinosaurus* and other sauropods remains a mystery. One explanation may be the increase in temperatures during the Mesozoic Era, as present-day reptiles living near the Equator tend to be larger than those in colder regions. It could also have been the result of feeding on plants that were low in nutrients. In order to digest them, sauropods would have needed to keep the vegetation in their stomachs and intestines for a long time. As they evolved, their bodies may have got bigger to fit their enlarged stomachs.

## COMPARING NEIGHBOURS

Of the nearly 60 species of sauropods, theropods and ornithischians found in Argentina, *Argentinosaurus* is one of the most famous. Its size makes it stand out among the dinosaurs.

Argentinosaurus

## PHYLOGENETIC TREE

| PERMIAN | 252 m.a. | TRIASSIC | 201 m.a. | JURASSIC | 145 m.a. | CRETACEOUS | 66 m.a. |
|---------|----------|----------|----------|----------|----------|------------|---------|

Sauropods

Titanosaurs

### THE RESEARCHERS
José Bonaparte and Rodolfo Coria wrote the scientific description and gave *Argentinosaurus* its name in 1993. The original fossils form part of the collections of the Museum Carmen Funes in Plaza Huincul.

### THE DISCOVERER
Guillermo Heredia found the remains of *Argentinosaurus* in 1989, while staying in Plaza Huincul. He immediately informed the local museum of palaeontology and helped to recover the fossil. Four years later, the actual value of his discovery would be known to all!

# Argentinosaurus

**LONG LEGS**
Only a few bones have been found,
including a fibula (lower leg) and
femur (thigh). The fibula was
1.55 m long and the femur would
have reached up to 2.4 m.

**TAIL**
The tail was not as long as in other sauropods.
It was very flexible and had more than 30
bones. Its flexibility may have meant that
*Argentinosaurus* could rear up on its hind legs
better than some of its sauropod relatives.

**WEIGHT SAVING**
In order to reduce the weight of the skeleton, the inner tissue of the spinal bone was spongy and had huge cavities, surrounded by very thin walls.

**SKELETON**
Scientists use comparisons with other more complete skeletons of similar dinosaurs to estimate *Argentinosaurus'* true size. *Argentinosaurus* may have been as long as three buses end to end.

# Finding Food

Dinosaurs developed varied adaptations in order to find food. The shape of their teeth, their stomach contents and fossilized faeces tell us about the kind of food they ate.

DRAGONFLY
Fossils show that insects such as dragonflies were present on the planet much earlier than dinosaurs. They were the main source of food for small flesh-eating animals, as they were plentiful and readily available.

The earliest dinosaurs appeared in small forms, some as small as chickens. These dinosaurs had tiny, pointed teeth and fed mainly on insects and other invertebrates they found among the plant leaves.

As the descendants of these dinosaurs grew bigger, they started to hunt larger animals. *Eoraptor* was the size of a turkey and may have fed on reptiles the size of lizards. *Herrerasaurus* reached 6 metres in length, and ate prey the size of wild boars.

In the Triassic Period, other small dinosaurs appeared that fed on a diet of insects, but later they replaced them with plants.

At the same time, the first gigantic (sauropodomorph) and bird-hipped (ornithischian) dinosaurs made their appearance. The sauropodomorphs soon reached the size of giraffes. Their necks increased in length, and they were able to get closer to high treetops to feed on leaves, branches and fruits. Ornithischians developed a beak and a complex set of teeth to help them grind their food.

**VELOCIRAPTOR** THE HUNTER
*Velociraptor* fought with larger animals, such as *Protoceratops*. It killed them with its curved claws and large, sharp teeth.

**SCIPIONYX**
*Scipionyx* was a small flesh-eating dinosaur from the Cretaceous Period. It captured insects and other invertebrates from plant leaves and shallow water.

**THEROPOD TEETH**
Theropods, such as *Velociraptor*, had razor-sharp teeth that were pointed and curved backwards.

**CURVED CLAWS**
The second toe on each of *Velociraptor*'s feet ended in a deadly sickle-shaped claw that it stuck into the bodies of its victims.

**STRANGE TEETH**
*Masiakasaurus* was a flesh-eating dinosaur from Madagascar with very odd teeth. It probably used them to poke into the bark of trees, searching for insects.

# Dinosaur Digestion

Most carnivorous and herbivorous dinosaurs did not chew their food. They used their teeth to rip and tear meat or plants. The mouthful was then swallowed and prepared for digestion in the stomach. The food was ground up in the gizzard, a muscular part of the stomach. Like present-day crocodiles and birds, dinosaurs swallowed stones. These stomach stones (gastroliths) helped to grind up food. They are commonly found in the ribcages of sauropod, ornithischian and theropod skeletons.

Ancient sauropods had spear-shaped teeth, while the teeth of the more advanced sauropods, such as *Diplodocus* (right) and *Nigersaurus,* were cylinder-shaped. They were long and slender like pegs and became very worn on the tip. This suggests that *Diplodocus* stripped the leaves from trees by pulling its teeth along a branch to gather just the leaves.

*Nigersaurus* had small teeth grouped together at the tip of a wide, spade-like snout. These teeth were useless for chewing. Instead, the dinosaurs nipped or stripped off leaves, then swallowed them.

The digestive system of flesh-eating dinosaurs was simpler than in herbivorous dinosaurs, as meat is easier to process than vegetable material. Therefore it is likely that the stomachs of carnivores were smaller than those of herbivores.

## DIGESTIVE SYSTEM OF HADROSAURS

Unlike most other herbivorous dinosaurs, the hadrosaurs ground up and chewed food in their mouths before swallowing it. They had hundreds of tiny teeth packed into groups, or batteries, which were constantly being replaced. Once swallowed, the vegetable material was further softened and broken up as it passed through the dinosaur's digestive system.

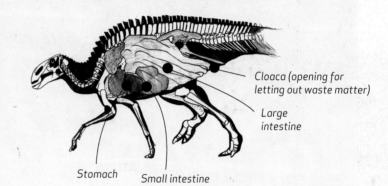

Cloaca (opening for letting out waste matter)

Large intestine

Stomach          Small intestine

**TEETH**
*Diplodocus* may have used its teeth to strip leaves and bark from trees in the same way that present-day giraffes do.

## COPROLITES AND GASTROLITHS

Fossilized faeces (coprolites) can help to identify the dinosaur that produced them by giving data about their feeding habits. They may contain fragments of seeds, leaves or sharp pieces of bone. Gastroliths are stones that help to break up food in the stomach.

*Coprolites*

*Gastroliths*

**WIDE SNOUT**
Some scientists think that *Diplodocus* may have also fed on softer water plants, its wide snout taking in vast quantities of food.

# Therizinosaurus

*Therizinosaurus* had a strong body, with long arms and two legs. There was doubt about its classification for years, because of its odd appearance. New finds of complete skeletons show that therizinosaurs were herbivorous theropods.

During the 1940s, palaeontologists from the USSR and Mongolia working together in the Gobi Desert discovered some very strange fossils. They were the front limbs of a reptile with amazingly long claws. For decades, the appearance of this animal and its relationship to other dinosaurs remained a mystery. However, the specimens were so large and interesting that eventually the appearance of this mysterious beast was reconstructed.

At first, the remains confused researchers when they tried to classify them. Russian palaeontologist Evgeny Maleev thought that they belonged to a turtle-like reptile. He gave it the name *Therizinosaurus* ('scythe lizard'). However, new samples found in 1950 helped palaeontologists to recognize it as a dinosaur. Several decades after its first discovery, it was classified as a theropod.

GENUS: THERIZINOSAURUS
CLASSIFICATION: SAURISCHIA, THEROPODA, THERIZINOSAURIDAE

**LENGTH** 10 m
**WEIGHT** 5000 kg
**DIET** Herbivorous

**STURDY ARM**
Each arm had a powerful muscle system, which continued up to the shoulder.

**LOCATION**
Remains of *Therizinosaurus* came from various rock formations in the region of the Gobi Desert, in Mongolia and China.

**PLANT DIET**
*Therizinosaurus* had a plant-based diet, even though it belonged to the same group as carnivorous dinosaurs such as *Velociraptor*.

**STRANGE FEATURES**
Despite being classified as a theropod, *Therizinosaurus* had a bird's hip, like the ornithischians, and four toes on each leg.

# Therizinosaurus

Although the known remains of *Therizinosaurus* are incomplete, it has been possible to do a reconstruction of its entire body from studies that compare it with other dinosaurs. It probably had a strong body, with a long neck ending in a small skull. Like the earliest bird-hipped dinosaurs, it moved on two legs, each ending in four toes. This was different from other theropods, which had only three toes.

*Therizinosaurus'* arms were up to 2.5 metres long, with three digits and an enormous claw on each one. It is possible the claws were up to 1 metre in length! Some palaeontologists believe they were used as weapons for defence, or in fights for territory. We also know now that *Therizinosaurus* was herbivorous, so it could have used its claws as a tool to cut the branches of trees, as present-day sloths do.

Some *Therizinosaurus* bones were discovered near fossilized eggs in 2013. These may have been from parents who looked after their eggs.

FIRST FINDINGS
Fossils of *Therizinosaurus* were discovered in 1948, in the Nemegt Formation of the Gobi Desert (see pages 88-89), in the south-west of Mongolia.

## CLOSE RELATIVES

Together with other species such as *Beipiaosaurus*, *Nothronychus* and *Alxasaurus*, *Therizinosaurus* formed a group that was defined only in the 1990s.

Alxasaurus          Nothronychus

Beipiaosaurus

## PHYLOGENETIC TREE

| PERMIAN | 252 m.a. | TRIASSIC | 201 m.a. | JURASSIC | 145 m.a. | CRETACEOUS | 66 m.a. |
|---------|----------|----------|----------|----------|----------|------------|---------|
| | | | | | | Therizinosaurs | |
| | | Theropods | | | Coelurosaurs | | |

## CLAWS

The largest of *Therizinosaurus'* three claws was on the first digit. These claws may have been used to cut leaves, branches and other vegetation.

Main claw

**BROAD BODY**
*Therizinosaurus* had a wide pelvis which probably meant it had a broad, deep body similar to that of present-day ostriches.

**DEADLY ATTACK**
*Therizinosaurus* was probably prey for *Tarbosaurus*. Even its amazing claws would have been little help against the attack of this fierce dinosaur.

# Therizinosaurus

**LONG AND SHORT**
We know the amazing length of *Therizinosaurus'* arms from the discovery of a complete set of fossil bones. Its legs and tail, however, were short compared to its arms.

**SKELETON**
The fossil remains of *Therizinosaurus* are incomplete. In order to reconstruct it, palaeontologists have studied dinosaurs such as *Erlikosaurus* and *Segnosaurus*.

**SKULL**
No fossil skull has been discovered for *Therizinosaurus*, so reconstruction of the head is based on palaeontologists' knowledge of similar dinosaurs.

**CLAWS**
*Therizinosaurus'* sharp claws are the longest known claws in an animal.

**HIP STRUCTURE**
*Therizinosaurus* had a hip structure similar to that of modern-day birds. It is possible that this shape helped to accommodate its long intestines.

# Dinosaur Families

Along with teeth, skeletons and footprints, a variety of fossilized dinosaur eggs, nests and embryos have been found. They have given us some surprising information about the early life of these animals.

Fossil remains show us that many dinosaurs nested in colonies. The eggs that have been found are of many different shapes and sizes.

Just as with present-day reptiles, the eggs had a protective shell. The tough outer shell explains how thousands of dinosaur eggs have been preserved as fossils.

The eggs were either covered by plants or incubated (kept warm so that they can develop) by the dinosaur parents. Parents may also have sat on their eggs in order to protect them from predators. We have learned a lot of information from discoveries of nests, with unhatched eggs and baby skeletons, belonging to the hadrosaur *Maiasaura*.

Baby *Maiasaura* dinosaurs would have fitted in the palm of a human hand! Their parents protected them and taught them where to go for food and water.

It is likely that dinosaurs could make sounds as signals to their young, just as birds do today, to create strong parental bonds.

## EGGS

The shape, size and colour of eggs varied according to the group of dinosaur.

*Chicken*

Velociraptor

Hypselosaurus

Oviraptor

Neuquensaurus

## HATCHING

The eggs of *Oviraptor* were almost 15 cm long! This reconstruction of an embryo that is about to hatch is based on the findings of hundreds of eggs in Cretaceous rocks from the Gobi Desert, Mongolia.

Oviraptor *embryo*

**BEAK**
*Maiasaura*'s wide beak helped it to transport large quantities of food to the nest.

**PROTECTIVE PARENTS**
After being born, the young remained in the nest, where adults fed them.

# Early Care

*Oviraptor* and *Velociraptor* dinosaurs incubated their young by sitting on top of their nests and controlling the temperature of the eggs directly with their own bodies. The first proof of this behaviour was seen in *Oviraptor* fossils in the Gobi Desert. The skeletons were found on top of their eggs, with their legs in the centre of the litter and their arms extended over the edges.

Skeleton of an *Oviraptor* sitting on its eggs and providing warmth for them.

## PROTOCERATOPS

*Protoceratops* was an ancient relative of *Triceratops*. Many specimens were discovered in Mongolia, which indicated they lived in herds. The young of this herbivore measured 17 cm, while the adults reached 2 m in length.

Parents took care of the newborn babies.

The nest consisted of a circular hollow in the sand.

## SNAKE THREAT

In India, the skeleton of a snake was found wrapped around a titanosaur nest! The snake could not have swallowed eggs, but it could have swallowed newborn babies.

**THE ARMS**
*Oviraptor* had feathered arms that helped to maintain the temperature of the eggs.

**FEEDING THEIR YOUNG**

A mother *Oviraptor* is shown regurgitating (bringing up) swallowed food to give to one of her young. Regurgitation helped to process and soften the food for the young to eat.

Dinosaur eggs

Snake

# Corythosaurus

*Corythosaurus* lived in large flocks in present-day Canada. It is a hadrosaur, or 'duck-billed' dinosaur, and its remains were found in rocks over 76 million years old.

Palaeontologist Barnum Brown gave *Corythosaurus* its name because its crest looked like the helmet of a Corinthian (ancient Greek) soldier! The North American palaeontologist found the first skeleton of *Corythosaurus* in the west of Canada. The skeleton that was uncovered was nearly complete; some fossilized skin was even preserved on one side.

Hadrosaurs formed the most successful herbivorous group at the end of the Cretaceous Period, mainly in North America and Asia, although fossils have been found in many parts of the world. Hadrosaurs had long snouts, rather like ducks' bills. Along their jaws were large numbers of teeth grouped in batteries, which they used to crush and grind vegetation. The most ancient hadrosaurs were the size of horses, but their descendants from the late Cretaceous Period grew to up to 10 metres in length!

We know about the hadrosaurs' diet from skeletons with preserved, fossilized plant remains in the stomach area. There are also fossilized faeces, which show that they ate leaves, fruits and seeds.

**LENGTH** 10 m
**WEIGHT** 4000 kg
**DIET** Herbivorous

GENUS: CORYTHOSAURUS
CLASSIFICATION: ORNITHISCHIA,
ORNITHOPODA, HADROSAURIDAE

**CRESTS**
The many species of hadrosaur can be recognized by the different structures of their crests.

**THE DISCOVERER**
In 1910, the American fossil hunter Barnum Brown led several successful expeditions in the west of Canada. There, the expeditions found a large variety of crest-headed hadrosaurs.

**DIET**
*Corythosaurus* raised itself up on its hind legs to eat leaves and fruits from conifers. It also ate ferns that it pulled out of the ground while walking on all four legs.

**LOCATION**
Hadrosaurs lived in large numbers in North America, but *Corythosaurus* has been found only in Canada.

Asia was home to many different hadrosaurs. Among them was the lambeosaurine (hadrosaurs with crests) *Aralosaurus*.

# Corythosaurus

The skull of *Corythosaurus* was notable not only for the long snout, but also for the large nose! The nostrils were lined with tissues that produced moisture and helped to trap particles from the air while *Corythosaurus* was breathing.

The hadrosaurs are divided into two families; those with hollow crests, such as *Corythosaurus*, are known as lambeosaurines. In the lambeosaurines, the nasal passages extended into the crests on the top of the head. Palaeontologists believe that by blowing air through the hollow passages in these crests, lambeosaurines could make loud sounds that would have carried over large distances. They probably helped to keep the lambeosaurines together and to send signals to warn of predators.

**LONG CREST**
*Parasaurolophus* was one of the most remarkable lambeosaurines, with an extra-long crest on its head!

**CHEWING**
Hadrosaurs had powerful jaw muscles that allowed them to crush and grind tough leaves and other vegetation.

## PHYLOGENETIC TREE

| PERMIAN | 252 m.a. | TRIASSIC | 201 m.a. | JURASSIC | 145 m.a. | CRETACEOUS | 66 m.a. |
|---------|----------|----------|----------|----------|----------|------------|---------|
| | | | | | | Hadrosaurs | |
| | | | | Ornithopods | | | |
| Ornithischians | | | | | | Iguanodonts | |

**SKELETON**

Vertebrae

Skull

Tail bones

**MALE CRESTS**
*Corythosaurus* males would have had larger crests than the female dinosaurs.

**FOOT STRUCTURE**
*Corythosaurus* had three thick toes that did not have claws, but ended in wide hooves. This foot structure helped the dinosaur to walk on all types of land surface.

# Corythosaurus

**SKIN**
The skin of *Corythosaurus* was covered by scales, spread evenly all over the body.

**BEHAVIOUR**
When feeding, *Corythosaurus* might have joined other herbivorous dinosaurs. These dinosaurs lived in herds and possibly moved regularly from one area to another.

**CREST SIZES**
The crest sizes would have varied depending on the gender and on the age of the animal.

**SHORT ARMS**
The arms were shorter than the legs. The study of footprints of hadrosaurs indicates that they walked mainly on four legs.

# Head Crests

In a Mesozoic world filled with predators and competitors, it was important for dinosaurs to be able to communicate and recognize each other. It was also vital that they could defend themselves.

**D**inosaurs developed a variety of structures to help them recognize each other as members of the same species. Head crests were one of these features.

Herbivorous beaked dinosaurs, such as *Triceratops,* had the most developed head crests of all, with huge horns and massive neck plates (see pages 134–139). The bird-like dinosaurs, such as *Parasaurolophus,* had hollow crests that allowed them to make deep sounds. These structures helped to identify the members of a group, but were not strong enough to defend the animals in fights. Pachycephalosaurs, however, had dome-shaped, thickened heads, which they may have used to defend themselves.

Some carnivorous theropods also developed odd-looking skulls. Early dinosaurs, such as *Dilophosaurus,* had crests on their heads. Later on in the Jurassic Period, both *Cryolophosaurus* and *Monolophosaurus* developed crests. We are still unsure today what these rather strange growths were used for.

In 2013, palaeontologists discovered skin impressions of a soft structure resembling a cockerel's wattle. These belonged to the hadrosaur *Edmontosaurus.*

**PACHYCEPHALOSAURUS**
This dinosaur lived at the end of the Cretaceous Period, together with *Triceratops* and *Tyrannosaurus rex.*

**HEAD**
A dome of solid bone and a row of spikes crowned the head of *Pachycephalosaurus.*

**COLOUR AND CAMOUFLAGE**

Body colour and patterns (camouflage) allow animals to blend in with their environment, making them difficult to spot. Scientists believe that dinosaurs also developed camouflage and other adaptations, according to the environment around them.

Antelope

Edmontosaurus

Dinosaurs living on plains may have had similar colours on their bodies to antelopes.

**CHASMOSAURUS**
The shape, design and colour of *Chasmosaurus*'s head allowed these animals to recognize other members of their herd.

Nasal openings

Hollow crest

**PARASAUROLOPHUS**

Lambeosaurine crests were connected to the nasal openings. Deep sounds are thought to have been produced when air was passed through them.

*Coelophysis* would have perhaps had stripes like a tiger, in order to hide among plants and trees.

Deer

Talenkauen

*Tiger*

Coelophysis

Some dinosaurs may have had light-coloured spots, rather like deer, to match the dappled (spotty) light in woods.

# Body Armour

Both the ankylosaurs and the stegosaurs developed bizarre body coverings for protection. These included spikes, plates and shields. Stegosaurs had a double row of plates running along the body, with a bunch of spikes at the end of the tail, which they used to defend themselves against predators and competitors. Ankylosaurs were four-legged, with low, strong bodies. They protected themselves from attack by resting their soft bellies on the ground. The spikes and plates on their backs saved them from the bites and scratches of their attackers.

The herbivorous dinosaurs *Amargasaurus* and *Agustinia* both had more complex bony formations on their backs for protection.

## AMARGASAURUS

The Argentinean palaeontologist José Bonaparte found this herbivorous dinosaur of the Cretaceous Period in Patagonia, Argentina, in 1991. From each of the vertebrae along its neck and back grew tall spines. Scientists are unsure what these spines were used for, but we know that they grew up to 80 centimetres in length along the dinosaur's neck. There were two rows of spines, which got smaller towards the back and became a single row near the hips.

## AGUSTINIA

*Agustinia* had a double set of long plates on top of its neck, back and tail. These plates helped to protect it from carnivores and were also used for recognition.

**SPINES**
Scientists have debated what these spines would have looked like in real life. They may have been covered in skin or horny growths. If more fossils are discovered in the future, then we may find out more information.

**BACK**
It's possible that *Amargasaurus* had a hump of fat along its raised back.

**SPIKED NECK**
When bending its neck downwards, the animal showed its great fan of spikes.

**HEAD**
*Amargasaurus* had a small head and thin teeth of cylindrical shape.

## PROTECTION AND RECOGNITION

The skulls of ankylosaurs were armour-plated and hardened, while some theropods had identifying crests.

*Euoplocephalus* and *Edmontonia* had hardened eyelids.

*Cryolophosaurus* had a fan-shaped crest.

*Citipati* had an unusually tall crest on top of its skull.

# Pachycephalosaurus

*Pachycephalosaur* means 'thick-headed reptile', and it is probable these dinosaurs used their tough heads to defend themselves.

**P**achycephalosaurus may be one of the most extraordinary-looking dinosaurs, with its domed skull and cone-shaped growths. It was two-legged, with long, strong hind legs and short front limbs. Its hips were wide, indicating that it had a large stomach that was able to contain and digest lots of vegetation.

The narrow beak at the end of the mouth had teeth of different shapes. At the upper tip of the snout, the teeth were cone-shaped and good for biting, whereas the ones at the sides of the cheek were leaf-shaped with saw-like edges. It is thought that pachycephalosaurs used their heads as powerful weapons in a fight. Their necks were strong, to withstand the impact of head-on collisions or side-swipes.

Pachycephalosaurs are closely related to the ceratopsians, so they are part of the Marginocephalia group. Dinosaurs in this group all have a skull with an outgrowth over the rear of the neck. In ceratopsians, this outgrowth consisted of delicate neck frills, but in pachycephalosaurs it was a series of cone-shaped knobs.

**TAIL**
*Pachycephalosaurus* had a very thick tail, with a mesh of tissues at the end to increase its strength.

GENUS: PACHYCEPHALOSAURUS
CLASSIFICATION: ORNITHISCHIA,
MARGINOCEPHALIA,
PACHYCEPHALOSAURIA

**SPEEDY**
With its long, powerful legs, *Pachycephalosaurus* could run at great speed.

**LENGTH** 4.5 m
**WEIGHT** 450 kg
**DIET** Herbivorous

**TEETH**
They were small but sharp, to cut tough plants and leaves.

**ARMS**
Its front limbs were a lot shorter than the back legs. Each one had five fingers ending in claws.

**LOCATION**
*Pachycephalosaurus* was identified in rocks from the end of the Cretaceous Period in the west of the United States.

Several species of pachycephalosaurs have been found in Cretaceous Period rocks from Mongolia.

# Pachycephalosaurus

During the last 20 million years of the Cretaceous Period, dinosaurs of the Marginocephalia group evolved in North America and Asia. *Pachycephalosaurus* and *Stegoceras* appeared in the west of the United States, and *Homocephale* and *Prenocephale* in the Gobi Desert of Mongolia.

*Pachycephalosaurus* was the largest member of Marginocephalia, measuring almost 4.5 metres long. The dome of the skull increased in height as the animal grew, and in males it was taller and more curved than in females.

*Pachycephalosaurus'* eyes were set inside large, deep cavities, which protected them during fights. The muscles of the neck were very powerful, and the backbone was built to withstand impacts. Its wide hips helped the animal to keep its balance.

## DIVERSITY OF PACHYCEPHALOSAURS

A large number of different skull types have been discovered in North America and Mongolia. Scientists debate whether these are all different species or whether they just represent different growth patterns in males and females. It was also announced in 2009 that two species of pachycephalosaurs were really just fossils of juveniles from other species.

Stygimoloch

Stegoceras

Goyocephale

## PHYLOGENETIC TREE

| PERMIAN | | TRIASSIC | | JURASSIC | | CRETACEOUS | |
|---|---|---|---|---|---|---|---|
| | 252 m.a. | | 201 m.a. | | 145 m.a. | | 66 m.a. |

Pachycephalosaurs

Marginocephalians

Ornithischians

Ceratopsians

**SKULL**
*Pachycephalosaurus* had a large skull with a dome about 25 cm in height, protecting a tiny brain!

# Pachycephalosaurus

**SKULL**
The skull was attached to the spine and neck with very strong muscles and tendons. This added strength must have been important to *Pachycephalosaurus*, but scientists are still unsure exactly how.

**HIPS**
The hips were wide, which has led some scientists to believe that these dinosaurs fought each other sideways-on.

**LEGS**
The shape of the bones show they were able to run fast and crash against an enemy.

**LONG BACKBONE**
It had long been thought that *Pachycephalosaurus* held its body straight, so that the shock of head-butting was absorbed along the whole length of the backbone. We know now that its neck was more of a U-shape, so this theory may no longer be true.

# Bird Evolution

Fossil history shows us the process of evolution that led to the development of birds from small feathered theropods, such as *Velociraptor*.

I t was the English naturalist Thomas Huxley who realized that the carnivorous *Compsognathus* and the oldest known bird, *Archaeopteryx*, shared the same type of back legs. This is how the theory that birds descended from dinosaurs was first developed.

The idea of a relationship between dinosaurs and birds was revived by palaeontologist John Ostrom (see page 126), with his discovery of the theropod *Deinonychus*. He found some extraordinary similarities between *Deinonychus* and *Archaeopteryx*.

In recent years, more evidence has been found to support the dinosaur–bird relationship. In China, palaeontologists discovered hundreds of rocks with complete specimens of *Caudipteryx* and *Microraptor*, which showed the presence of different types of feathers. In Mongolia, they found skeletons of *Oviraptors* sitting on their eggs. However, it is *Unenlagia* ('half-bird') that is the most bird-like dinosaur found so far.

**CONFUCIUSORNIS**
The first birds, such as *Confuciusornis*, had teeth and were roughly the size of pigeons.

**LONG STEPS**
The femur (thigh bone) was adapted for running.

## ARMS INTO WINGS

The lengthening of the arms and their feathers, together with the ability to flap with force, led to the appearance of wings.

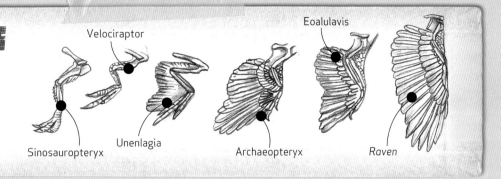

Velociraptor

Eoalulavis

Sinosauropteryx

Unenlagia

Archaeopteryx

Raven

**FEATHERED ARMS**
*Unenlagia* was able to flap its arms, but it could not fly!

**TEARING TEETH**
*Unenlagia*'s small teeth were useful for tearing, but not for chewing food.

**ACTIVE HUNTERS**
With the help of their large eyes and brains, avian (bird-like) theropods could judge the movement and distance of their prey.

**SKELETON**
*Unenlagia*'s long arms show the stage from which the wings of ancient birds, such as *Archaeopteryx*, developed. The second toes of its feet had large, sickle-shaped claws, which were used for hunting and fighting.

**TAIL**
The tail had 16 bones.

**THORAX**
The fused furcula or 'wishbone'.

**BONES**
The bones were hollow to reduce weight.

**ARMS**
The first digit (finger) of the arms was shortened – a feature of wings.

# Bird Evolution

The skeleton of *Unenlagia* was found in Cretaceous Period rocks from Patagonia, Argentina. The fossil shows us that the arms of these advanced theropods moved in the same way as birds' wings. The body structure of *Unenlagia* indicates that this animal was at a development stage between theropods, such as *Deinonychus,* and ancient birds, such as *Archaeopteryx.*

Until quite recently, no Mesozoic fossils with feathers had been found since *Archaeopteryx,* in 1862. However, since the 1990s, a number of small dinosaurs with feathered bodies have been discovered in Liaoning, China. These fossils were preserved very well in soft mud in a lake from the Early Cretaceous Period.

## MICRORAPTOR

The majority of dinosaurs with feathers are included in the group Maniraptora. Small forms, such as *Dilong,* had well-developed feathers, but other big forms, such as *Tyrannosaurus,* did not have them. *Microraptor* was a bit less than 1 metre long and was a relative of *Deinonychus* and *Unenlagia.* It had four wings! Its front limbs and back legs had long, wide feathers that helped it to glide and fly. *Microraptor* threw itself from trees, then used its front wings to glide and possibly flap, and its back wings to control its motion – like a rudder. The contents of its stomach showed that it hunted tiny mammals.

### EGG-SITTER
Birds got the habit of sitting on their nests to protect and provide warmth to their eggs from their theropod ancestors, such as *Oviraptor.*

## FOSSILIZED BEHAVIOUR

The fossilized skeleton of the small theropod *Mei long* ('sleeping dragon') was found sitting on its heels, with its tail and neck around the body, and the snout under one arm. This position is similar to the one used by modern-day birds to keep warm and to rest.

*Fossilized skeleton*

*Reconstruction*

### HIND FEATHERS
These feathers were used as a rudder to control the direction of flight.

**CLUSTER OF FEATHERS**
The pattern of feathers on the body of a dinosaur or bird are often preserved in fossils too, showing where clumps of feathers grew or crests on the head were formed, for example.

**FRONT WINGS**
These were used for gliding and perhaps for flapping.

**CLAWS**
*Microraptor* clung to branches with its claws.

**FEATHERED DINOSAURS**
As a result of new discoveries, especially in China, there is now direct fossil evidence for feathers in at least 40 different species of dinosaur. Due to this, scientists now agree that there is an evolutionary link between birds and dinosaurs.

Unenlagia

# Caudipteryx

*Caudipteryx* had small wing-like arms with claws. The feathers in its tail balanced the body and were used to identify it to other members of the same species.

C*audipteryx* ('tail with feathers') was a species of *Oviraptor* about the same size as a present-day turkey. It was mainly a carnivorous dinosaur but it had omnivorous habits – it fed on both invertebrate animals and vegetation. Its head was small and high, with large eyes. It had a short snout with a horny beak and a few tiny, pointed teeth at the end. Some specimens of *Caudipteryx* have gastroliths (stomach stones) in the area of the gizzard, which indicates that it may also have eaten some seeds.

The fossils of this theropod show that the body was covered by short feathers which controlled its body temperature. Its arms were covered by longer feathers; however, these small wings were not fit for flying. The wing-like arms and the feathers at the tip of the tail helped to balance the body when the animal was running, especially when it was turning.

GENUS: CAUDIPTERYX
CLASSIFICATION: SAURISCHIA, THEROPODA, MANIRAPTORA

**SPEEDY RUNNER**
The long legs, similar to those of a South American rhea, show that *Caudipteryx* was a fast runner.

**LENGTH** 1 m
**WEIGHT** 3 kg
**DIET** Omnivorous

**MOBILITY**
The thin, flexible neck might have helped *Caudipteryx* to gather food.

**DIET**
With its narrow beak, *Caudipteryx* caught small invertebrates that were found in the bark of trees.

**LOCATION**
Maniraptor fossils have been found around the world. *Deinonychus* was discovered in the United States, and *Unenlagia* in Argentina.

*Caudipteryx* was found in Liaoning, China, together with fossils of other dinosaurs with feathers.

# Caudipteryx

The maniraptors ('seizing hands') are the theropod dinosaurs most closely related to birds. Their hands had three long fingers that ended in curved, pointed claws. The arms of these dinosaurs generally bent in a zigzag shape. They had a system of tissues and joints that made their hands automatically extend forwards when stretching their arms. This feature is also shared by birds.

Among the most important maniraptors were oviraptors (such as *Caudipteryx*), therizinosaurs and the alvarezsaurs (insect-eaters with tiny arms, such as *Alvarezsaurus*, *Patagonykus* and *Mononykus*).

The main group of maniraptors was the deinonychosaurs. Their name ('terrible or fearsome claw') refers to the large sickle-shaped claws on the second toes of their feet. These hunters ate all types of food, according to their body sizes: the tiny *Microraptor* hunted small mammals; *Velociraptor* preyed on bigger dinosaurs, such as *Protoceratops*; and *Austroraptor* hunted titanosaurs the size of present-day hippopotamuses.

**CHINESE SKELETONS**
The dinosaur specimens from Liaoning, China, are preserved in rocks that are around 125 million years old. The rock layers where *Caudipteryx* was found also contained remains of other feathered dinosaurs, such as *Dilong* and *Sinornithosaurus*.

**BIRD-LIKE**

The maniraptors include a large variety of bird-like theropods, with a variety of diets and a range of different levels of development in their arms.

Beipiaosaurus

Mononykus

Similicaudipteryx

## PHYLOGENETIC TREE

| PERMIAN | 252 m.a. | TRIASSIC | 201 m.a. | JURASSIC | 145 m.a. | CRETACEOUS | 66 m.a. |
|---------|----------|----------|----------|----------|----------|------------|---------|
| | | | | | | Oviraptors | |
| | | | | Coelurosaurs | | | |
| | | | Tetanurans | | | Therizinosaurs | |
| | Theropods | | | | | | |

**COURTING**
*Caudipteryx* may have showed off its colourful feathers to possible mates with repetitive body movements.

**INCISIVOSAURUS**
This cousin of *Caudipteryx* had large teeth at the tip of its snout, similar to those of rodents. The skull measured 10 cm.

# Caudipteryx

**NECK**
The neck had a large number of bones, making movement easy.

**SKELETON**
The skeleton was adapted for swift movement.

**HIND LEGS**
*Caudipteryx* had long, slim legs. It could run quickly when chased by predators.

**SKULL**
It was small but tall. It had big eyes and a thin rough snout that was covered by a horny beak.

**FEATHERED TAIL**
The marks of the skin show that the feathers were arranged in a fan shape at the tip of the tail.

# PREHISTORIC REPTILES

During the Mesozoic Era, a wide variety of reptiles existed alongside the dinosaurs. Many of these reptiles reached gigantic sizes.

# Life in the Depths

During the Mesozoic Era, dinosaurs ruled the land. But in the seas and oceans, reptiles that were distantly related to dinosaurs dominated the water.

**ARCHELON**
*Archelon* was a huge sea turtle that appeared in the seas around North America approximately 70 million years ago. It measured 4 metres in diameter! Theropod dinosaurs fed on its eggs, which it laid on beaches.

A variety of animals lived in the seas during the Mesozoic Era. Many groups of invertebrates appeared in Panthalassa, the ocean surrounding the supercontinent of Pangea. They included jellyfish, corals, ammonites, oysters, sea urchins, sea lilies and lobsters. Alongside these invertebrates were different types of fish and reptiles, such as ichthyosaurs (which looked like dolphins), plesiosaurs, mosasaurs and different species of crocodile. These reptiles formed part of a process of evolution that is often called the Mesozoic 'marine revolution'. This event began around 150 million years ago and gave rise to a large variety of animal life.

Even though certain reptiles had their origins on land, they adapted successfully to life underwater. This was possible thanks to changes in their bodies, which allowed them to move smoothly underwater, as well as changes to their lungs. Plesiosaurs, for example, evolved flipper-like limbs to help them swim efficiently.

**PREDATORS**
Plesiosaurs were some of the largest predators in the oceans and lakes.

Ichthyosaurus

Human

Mosasaurus

Elasmosaurus

Plesiosaurus

## SEA REPTILES

Plesiosaurs, ichthyosaurs and mosasaurs were all sea reptiles that lived during the Mesozoic Era.

## ELASMOSAURUS

*Elasmosaurus* had an extremely long neck made up of more than 70 bones.

## THE ORIGIN OF FLIPPERS

The plesiosaurs are included in the group Sauropterygia ('lizard flippers'). The oldest of this group did not have flippers, but their fingers were connected by a thin layer of skin that helped them to move in the water.

Humerus (bone in upper arm)

Ulna (bone in lower arm)

Radius (bone in lower arm)

Humerus

Ulna

Radius

PACHYPLEUROSAURS

NOTHOSAURS

EARLY PLESIOSAURS

LATE PLESIOSAURS

## LONG NECK

Although it could twist its long neck to and fro, *Elasmosaurus* did not have the flexibility of modern-day tortoises or snakes.

# Liopleurodon

*Liopleurodon* was one of the main sea predators in the Jurassic Period, with needle-sharp teeth and powerful jaws.

This enormous plesiosaur is one of the most fascinating sea reptiles due to its huge size and its body structure. It lived during the Jurassic Period in the region that is now Europe. *Liopleurodon* was a type of pliosaur (short-necked plesiosaur). It had a huge head, a strong body suited to moving smoothly under water, and four flippers.

The first example of this huge reptile was part of a single tooth found in northern France. It was described by the French palaeontologist Henri Émile Sauvage in 1873. He noticed that the tooth had ridges or marks on one side, while the other side was completely smooth. Because of this, and the discovery of other teeth, he called this creature *Liopleurodon* ('smooth-sided tooth'). Since then, more remains have been found, including parts of skeletons of *Liopleurodon ferox*, as well as at least two other species, *Liopleurodon pachydeirus* and *Liopleurodon rossicus*.

**LAND TO SEA**
The ancestors of *Liopleurodon* were land reptiles. But, as they adapted to living underwater, their legs gradually became paddle-shaped.

GENUS: LIOPLEURODON
CLASSIFICATION: PLESIOSAURIA,
PLIOSAUROIDEA, PLIOSAURIDAE

**LENGTH** 6–10.5 m
**WEIGHT** 5000 kg
**DIET** Carnivorous

**TEETH**
Each jawbone had up to 28
circular teeth, with three
sides in cross-section,
held by long, strong roots.

**LOCATION**
Remains of *Liopleurodon
ferox* have been found
in France, Germany and
England. *Liopleurodon
pachydeirus* was discovered
in England, and *Liopleurodon
rossicus* in Russia.

# Liopleurodon

The exact size of these animals has always been based on guesswork because *Liopleurodon* skeletons have only been found in pieces. The largest skull of *Liopleurodon* found so far is around 1.5 metres long. Therefore, it has been estimated that the total body length must have been between 6 and 10.5 metres. These observations also match the size of bite marks recorded on the bones of *Liopleurodon*'s prey.

In 2002, pieces of a giant fossilized skeleton found in Mexico, near the town of Aramberri, were given the name 'Monster of Aramberri' by the media. The skeleton is possibly a pliosaur and was originally thought to be *Liopleurodon*, although this is now considered unlikely. Reports of its possible size became wildly exaggerated!

Pliosaur fossils uncovered in the Svalbard group of islands in Norway were given the names 'The Monster' and 'Predator X' when they hit the headlines in 2007 and 2009. It's thought that these beasts could have been up to 15 metres long.

FIRST DISCOVERIES
The first specimens of *Liopleurodon* were found in brick pits in both France and England. They included the famous Oxford clay quarries near Peterborough, where many specimens from the Middle Jurassic Period have been found.

## PHYLOGENETIC TREE

| PERMIAN | 252 m.a. | TRIASSIC | 201 m.a. | JURASSIC | 145 m.a. | CRETACEOUS | 66 m.a. |
|---------|----------|----------|----------|----------|----------|------------|---------|
| | | | | Pliosaurs | | *Liopleurodon* | |

Plesiosaurs

## TAKEN BY SURPRISE

*Liopleurodon* had five to seven pairs of long, sharp teeth jutting out from the tip of its mouth, and many more in each full jawbone. The teeth are quite similar to those of killer whales, so they could have had certain feeding habits in common, such as cooperative hunting and surprise beach attacks on prey.

### THE ATTACK

It could move at great speed to attack and kill its prey, through short and quick movements of its limbs.

# Liopleurodon

**HEAD**
*Liopleurodon* had a flattened, triangle-shaped head, rather like the head of a crocodile. Once it had its prey in its jaws, it might have twisted and spun until chunks of meat could be torn off and swallowed whole.

**DEADLY STRUCTURE**
The triangle-shaped skull, with deep-rooted teeth, allowed *Liopleurodon* to tear flesh from its victims.

**REPRODUCTION**
It's possible that *Liopleurodon* gave birth to a single, large baby, which then received the full care of its mother.

**FLIPPER MOVEMENT**
*Liopleurodon* had long, wide flippers with powerful muscles. As the pliosaur moved through the water, it performed alternating movements between the front and rear flippers.

**GASTROLITHS**
We know that *Liopleurodon* swallowed stones (gastroliths) to help it grind and digest its food.

# Flying Lizards

Pterosaurs were the first vertebrate animals to fly. They inhabited a great variety of oceans and continents. But although pterosaurs appeared in many forms and adapted in an extraordinary way, they disappeared without leaving any descendants.

**FRAGILE AND DELICATE**
Pterosaurs had light, hollow bones, which made their fossilization difficult. There were very few early discoveries, and therefore little detailed knowledge of these animals. Now scientists have plenty of good fossils to study, and we know much more than we did.

The name *pterosaur* means 'winged lizard'. They lived during the Mesozoic Era, from around 225 million years ago to the end of the Cretaceous Period, 66 million years ago. Pterosaurs were flying reptiles with forelimbs that were evolved into wings. The fourth finger was extremely long and supported an elastic skin structure (membrane) that was linked to the body.

Pterosaurs are close relatives of dinosaurs, but fossils of their ancestors are not known. It is thought that these ancestors must have been tree-living reptiles with skin folds, which they used to help them glide.

In 1767, the first pterosaur remains were found in Germany. Since then, there have been many different theories about these animals – even the possibility that they were swimmers. But today, we know they were accomplished fliers.

Together with birds and bats, pterosaurs are the only flying vertebrate animals known. Powerful flying muscles were attached to their breastbones. The species that lived in more open spaces had long, narrow wings to help them glide. However, those living in woods or rocky areas had short, wide wings for more flexible movement.

## FLIGHT

### TAKING OFF
They launched themselves from high places or jumped.

### LANDING
They landed on their hind legs, and then balanced themselves.

### DIET
Pterosaurs caught fish by flying low across water. Some species also fed on fruit, insects, vertebrates and dead animals (carrion).

### THE SANTANA FORMATION
During the Late Cretaceous Period in Brazil, several species of pterosaur lived together on the shores of shallow water. Many of their fossils have been found in deposits known as the Santana Formation (named after a nearby village).

# Pteranodon

*Pteranodon* was a flying reptile with wings and a toothless beak. Its name actually means 'winged and toothless'!

This pterosaur lived at the end of the Cretaceous Period in North America. The males measured about six metres from the tip of one wing to the tip of the other. *Pteranodon* was well adapted for flying and probably caught fish from the surface of the water while skimming above it. This flying reptile might have lived in crowded groups (colonies) on rocky islands, where it nested.

Unlike its ancient relatives, the rhamphorhynchoids of the Jurassic Period, *Pteranodon* did not have any teeth. It did, however, have a crest. These helped them to recognize each other and to attract mates. Adult males had crests that pointed backwards over the head, while females' crests were less developed. The females were generally smaller than the males, with wing spans of about 3 metres.

Although they emerged from common ancestors, pterosaurs are not dinosaurs or birds. In pterosaurs, the wing is formed from a membrane (a thin layer of skin) that is supported by an extra-long fourth finger. Birds do not have a membrane or a fourth finger.

In 2011, scientists discovered a fossil of the pterosaur *Darwinopterus* in north-eastern China. It shows an adult skeleton fossilized in the act of laying an egg!

GENUS: PTERANODON
CLASSIFICATION: PTEROSAURIA,
PTERODACTYLOIDEA,
PTERANODONTIDAE

LENGTH 6 m
WEIGHT 50 kg
DIET Piscivorous
(mainly a fish eater)

### ANUROGNATHUS

*Anurognathus* was a small pterosaur that lived at the end of the Jurassic Period. It had a wing span of up to 50 cm and fed on flying insects.

### MOVING ABOUT

*Pteranodon* was built for flight and was very clumsy on land. Although it was able to move on all four limbs, its hind legs were small and very weak, so it would not have been able to run.

### LOCATION

*Pteranodon* has been found only in the central region of North America.

Finds of pterosaurs in Asia are thought to make up the family Azhdarchidae. They include *Zhejiangopterus* from China and *Azhdarcho* from Uzbekistan.

# Pteranodon

The most ancient ancestors of the pterosaurs, the rhamphorhynchoids, appeared in the Triassic Period. They had beaked snouts, pointed teeth and a long tail ending in a diamond-shaped flap of skin. Other ancestors were the pterodactyloids ('winged finger') that appeared in the Jurassic Period. The rhamphorhynchoids did not survive to the Cretaceous Period, but the pterodactyloids survived to become the most common flyers of the Mesozoic Era. Pterodactyloids had shorter tails, larger heads and much longer and more flexible necks than the rhamphorhynchoids.

**SKULL OF *PTERANODON***
A fossilized bolus (rounded mass of chewed food), formed of fish bones, was found inside one specimen's beak.

**FEEDING ITS YOUNG**
*Pteranodon* stored fish in its crop (a pouch near the throat) in order to transport food to the nest, where its hungry babies waited!

**GIANT PTEROSAURS**
Azhdarchids, such as *Quetzalcoatlus*, were the largest flying creatures of all time, with a wingspan of 11 m! They walked on four legs and kept their necks straight. They looked similar to present-day giraffes.

## PHYLOGENETIC TREE

| PERMIAN | 252 m.a. | TRIASSIC | 201 m.a. | JURASSIC | 145 m.a. | CRETACEOUS | 66 m.a. |
|---------|----------|----------|----------|----------|----------|------------|---------|

Pterosaurs

Archosaurs

Dinosaurs

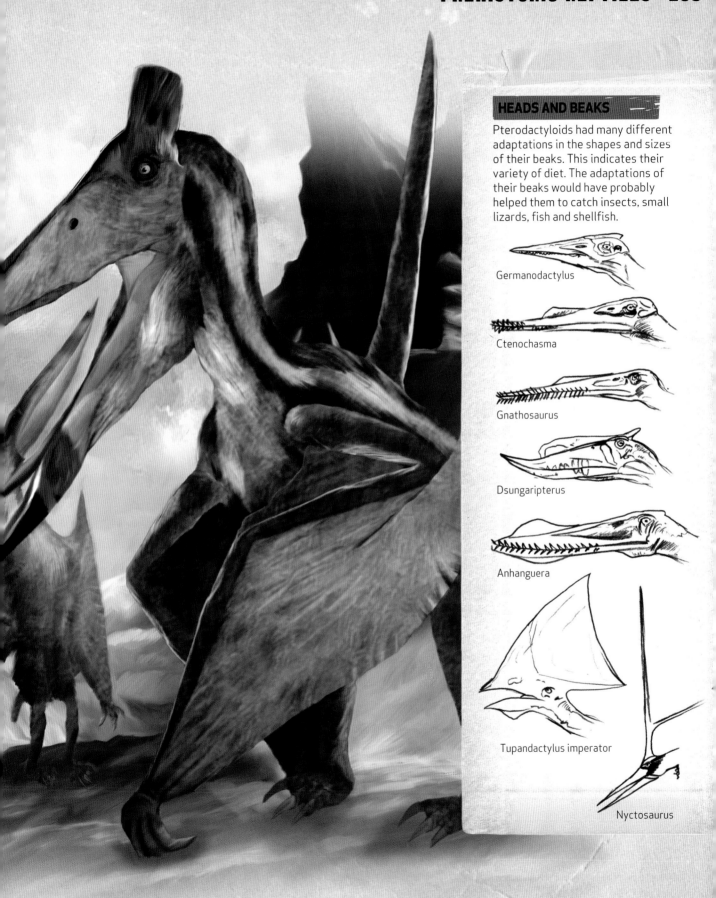

## HEADS AND BEAKS

Pterodactyloids had many different adaptations in the shapes and sizes of their beaks. This indicates their variety of diet. The adaptations of their beaks would have probably helped them to catch insects, small lizards, fish and shellfish.

Germanodactylus

Ctenochasma

Gnathosaurus

Dsungaripterus

Anhanguera

Tupandactylus imperator

Nyctosaurus

# Pteranodon

**POSTURE**
On land, pterosaurs moved on four limbs. They folded their wings so that the four fingers pointed upwards, to avoid them hitting the ground.

**HANDS**
Pterosaurs had three inner fingers on their hands, all with claws. An extra bone, the pteroid, served as support for the front region of the wing.

**CRESTS**
The most distinctive feature of *Pteranodon* skulls was the crest. This was a bony outgrowth which varied in shape depending on age, sex and species. These crests might have been colourful and were connected to the neck through skin folds.

**SKELETON**
The bones were hollow to reduce body weight. The neck was flexible and the tail quite short.

**WINGS**
The wings were formed by a wide membrane of flexible, rough skin, which was supported by the fourth, extremely long finger on each hand. This membrane was connected to the hind legs.

# THE END
## OF AN ERA

Around 66 million years ago, the dinosaurs, along with a large number of other vertebrates, suddenly disappeared. There is much debate about what led to this mass extinction.

# The Mystery of Extinction

Dinosaurs appeared in the Triassic Period, taking the place of synapsids and other ancient reptiles. In the Jurassic Period, they developed to huge sizes and, in the Cretaceous Period, they were widespread and dominant – until they mysteriously disappeared.

The Mesozoic Era started 252 million years ago, after a great extinction removed most of the synapsids from the Paleozoic Era. During the Mesozoic, the most varied, common and gigantic vertebrates were the reptiles. This group included sea animals, land animals, such as dinosaurs and crocodiles, and flying animals, including pterosaurs and birds.

The Mesozoic Era finished 66 million years ago in the same way it had started – with a major extinction. The great disappearance at the end of the Cretaceous Period left the Earth with almost no large animals!

There are many theories to explain why this happened. One of the most popular is that the Earth was struck by a large meteorite (a piece of rock from space). Although nothing has been proven, what we do know for certain is that a catastrophic event caused the disappearance of many species on land and in the sea, bringing to an end the 'golden age' of the reptiles.

## LETHAL IMPACT

It is believed that a large meteorite struck the Earth and its impact released large quantities of dust and vapour, which would have caused climate change on a global scale. Other theories suggest that a volcanic eruption may have caused a great release of gases and ash. The result would have been a drop in world temperatures and the formation of acid rain. In the long term, the dust and ash could have led to a greenhouse effect (a warming up of the layer of gases around Earth), which would have reduced the amount of sunlight reaching Earth and caused many animals and plants to die.

LAYER OF IRIDIUM
The unusual amount of this rare chemical element found in rocks dating from the end of the Cretaceous Period supports the idea of a meteorite hitting the Earth.

BEE FOSSIL
Many groups of animals, including insects, managed to survive the destruction.

## THE CHICXULUB CRATER

A crater in the Yucatán Peninsula, Mexico, was produced by a meteorite of around 10 km in diameter that hit the Earth at the end of the Cretaceous Period. Scientists believe this impact may have caused the extinction of the dinosaurs.

Mexico

Gulf of Mexico

Yucatán °

# Pleistocene Giants

Large animals, typically weighing several hundred kilograms, increased in number around the middle and end of the Cenozoic Era. They are known as megafauna. They too disappeared suddenly around 50,000 years ago, for reasons that have not yet been explained.

The Pleistocene Epoch is the last major division of the Cenozoic Era (see page 11). It started approximately 2.5 million years ago. During this time, several ice ages occurred that gave rise to a cold, dry climate in which gigantic animals (megafauna) developed.

Huge mammoths and mastodons, larger than present-day elephants, appeared alongside giant deer with antlers of up to 3.5 metres, woolly rhinoceroses and cave bears. The huge size of many species might have been due to them having stores of fat to avoid heat loss in the cold climate.

During this period, both South America and Australia separated from the other land masses. This caused their animal life to develop in different ways from elsewhere on the planet. Animals such as kangaroos evolved, but in Australia they grew to gigantic sizes! Some groups of animals developed only in South America. They included xenarthrans, represented today by armadillos, tree sloths and anteaters. Other giant South American animals included ground sloths, such as *Glossotherium*, *Lestodon* and *Megatherium*.

**SIZE**
The largest mammoth reached 4 m in height and 9 tonnes in weight, though some males might have been bigger!

**MAMMOTH**
The mammoth was related to present-day elephants.

## DIVERSITY

Some of the megafauna species, such as the glyptodonts, have descendants among present-day animals. Others, such as *Macrauchenia*, did not leave any descendants.

Macrauchenia

Glyptodon

Toxodon

# Pleistocene Giants

Around 50,000 years ago, Europe and Asia lost more than a third of their large mammals, and North America lost nearly three-quarters! In South America, all of the megafauna disappeared. These mass extinctions happened at the same time as a decrease in the temperature of the planet, which might have affected these animals. At the same time, human species increased in number on every continent. It is possible that humans over-hunted many of these giant animals. However, it is likely that each species died out for different reasons.

## MEGAFAUNA IN AUSTRALIA

None of the large species that lived in Australia nearly 50,000 years ago still exist today. Many megafauna fossils have been discovered at the Naracoorte Caves site, located in southern Australia. Skeletons of species found there include *Procoptodon*, *Diprotodon* and *Thylacoleo*.

### THYLACOLEO

*Thylacoleo* was a marsupial lion (a lion with a pouch). It was a predator the size of a leopard that could weigh 150 kg.

## STRANGE SET OF TEETH

The teeth of *Thylacoleo* had similarities with those of herbivorous species. But its pointed, razor-sharp back teeth were suited to a meat diet. This is similar to the teeth of present-day cats, which are also adapted for a carnivorous diet.

Thylacoleo
(marsupial)

Present-day cat

### MEGALANIA
The huge *Megalania* was a relative of present-day large reptiles such as Komodo dragons and monitor lizards. It could reach 7 m in length and exceed half a tonne in weight!

**FEATHERED GIANT**

*Genyornis* was a non-flying bird that reached 2.5 m in height. It hunted animals for food, but it was also a scavenger that ate any leftovers it could find!

### PROCOPTODON
*Procoptodon* was the largest kangaroo that ever existed. Its face was small and its arms long, with claws.

### DIPROTODON
Weighing around 2.8 tonnes, *Diprotodon* was the largest marsupial that ever existed. It was the size of a rhinoceros.

# Smilodon

*Smilodon* had big, cone-shaped canine teeth from which it got its scientific name, meaning 'carving knife tooth'. Its body was well adapted for eating large prey.

S*milodon* lived in the Pleistocene Epoch. Three different species have been found across North and South America.

*Smilodon* was similar in size to an African lion, although it had a stronger body. Its tail was only a few centimetres long, like a lynx's tail. Its teeth were adapted to suit a carnivorous diet. The cheekbones were wide, containing powerful chewing muscles. Its canines were extremely long and flattened, with a saw-like rear edge. Each one was more than 15 centimetres in length!

*Smilodon* could open its jaws very wide to allow its long teeth to pierce the skin and muscles of its prey. It also had strong muscles in its neck and shoulders, which helped it to attack its victims with great force. This meant it could kill and eat animals much larger than itself.

Among its prey were large mammals, including giant ground sloths, bison, horses, deer, and the young of mastodons and mammoths.

**LENGTH** 2 m
**WEIGHT** 400 kg
**DIET** Carnivorous

GENUS: SMILODON
CLASSIFICATION: CARNIVORE, FELIDAE, MACHAIRODONTINAE

**HUGE CANINES**
Unlike those of modern-day cats, *Smilodon*'s massive canine teeth were curved and oval-shaped.

**DEADLY BITE**
After bringing its prey under control with its front legs, *Smilodon* would inflict a wound with the help of its canines. Then it would wait for its prey to bleed to death.

**LOCATION**
*Smilodon populator* lived in South America. Specimens have been found in Brazil, Argentina, Venezuela, Ecuador, Bolivia, Chile and Uruguay. *Smilodon fatalis* lived mainly in North America. *Smilodon gracilis* was found in the south-east of the United States.

**LIMBS**
*Smilodon* had strong front legs, with large claws that could be drawn in or extended. These vicious claws helped it to injure and limit the movement of its prey.

# Smilodon

**HERDS**
It is not clear whether *Smilodon* lived in groups or alone. Some specimens indicate that individuals affected by illness were helped or looked after by other members of a group.

**HIPS**
*Smilodon* had wide hips that contained the large muscles of the legs. These muscles balanced the animal when fighting.

**CAMOUFLAGE**
*Smilodon*'s short back legs and small tail indicate it was a predator that attacked suddenly. In order to get close and jump on its prey, it must have hidden. For this reason, it is thought that it might have had spots as camouflage.

**SAW-TOOTHED**
*Smilodon* had small, pointed outgrowths of enamel (the hard outer layer of a tooth), which gave its teeth a slightly saw-like appearance.

# Glossary

**algae** Organisms that live mostly in water and range from tiny forms to giant seaweeds.

**amniotes** Creatures (with limbs and backbones) that lay eggs; they include reptiles, birds and mammals.

**amphibian** A vertebrate animal that is adapted to live both on land and in water.

**anatomy** Structure of a living thing.

**ankylosaurs** Armoured dinosaurs from the early Jurassic and Cretaceous Periods.

**Araucaria** An evergreen coniferous tree, which has survived to modern times as a 'living fossil'.

**arthropods** Invertebrate animals that have hard, jointed outer skeletons. They include lobsters, crabs, spiders and centipedes.

**asphalt** A natural sticky, black liquid that is a form of petroleum. In some places it seeps from under the ground to the surface to form 'tar pits'.

**bacteria** Tiny, single-celled organisms that live in almost every environment on Earth.

**bipedal** Describes an animal that moves on two feet.

**camouflage** Body colours and patterns that allow animals to blend with their environment, making them difficult to spot.

**canine teeth** Long teeth at either side of the mouth, like fangs.

**carnivore** An organism that gets its main source of nutrition from animal flesh (a meat-eater).

**carrion** Dead animals, often eaten by scavengers.

**cartilage** A flexible, elastic-like tissue that exists in bodies of animals to connect joints and other parts.

**cavity** A hole.

**cephalopod** Type of mollusc that lives in water and typically has arms or tentacles. They include squid, cuttlefish and octopuses.

**ceratopsians** Herbivorous, beaked dinosaurs that flourished during the Cretaceous Period, including *Triceratops*.

**cold-blooded** Describes animals in which the body temperature varies according to the surrounding air temperature: frogs and toads, for example.

**conifer** A tree with needle-shaped leaves and seeds attached to cones. Most conifers are evergreen (they do not shed their leaves).

**coprolite** Fossilized faeces.

**crop** Birds, some dinosaurs and a few other animals have this pouch near the throat for the storage of food before digestion.

**cycad** A seed plant that typically has a wood stem with a crown of tough, evergreen leaves.

**cynodonts** Mammal-like reptiles that first appeared in the Late Permian Period.

**embryo** The early stage of an animal while it is in the egg, or in the womb of its mother.

**evolution** The process of gradual change and adaptation of life forms over successive generations.

**extinction** The dying out of a species.

**faeces** Solid waste product from an animal.

**fossil** A trace of an organism that has been preserved from prehistoric times. Solid parts of animals, such as shells, teeth or bones, change into a stony substance over millions of years in a process called fossilization. Fossils may also be marks left behind by an organism, such as footprints, faeces (coprolites), or patterns (impressions) left by skin texture.

**gastrolith** A stone deliberately swallowed by some animals in order to help grind up food in the digestive system. Some dinosaur fossils have been found with gastroliths.

**gills** Organs found in organisms that live in water which allow them to 'breathe' by getting oxygen from the surrounding water and excreting (giving out) carbon dioxide.

**ginkgo** A non-flowering plant that dates back around 270 million years, making it a 'living fossil'.

**gizzard** The muscular part of the stomach in birds and some other animals where food is broken down for digestion.

**hadrosaurs** Duck-billed dinosaurs belonging to the order Ornithischia.

**herbivore** An animal that obtains its nutrients from plants and other vegetation (a plant-eater).

**ice ages** Also known as glacial ages. Times in the Earth's geological history when global temperatures have dropped, and large areas of the Earth's surface have been covered in ice sheets. There have been several ice ages in Earth's history, some lasting for several million years. The most recent major ice age ended about 11,700 years ago.

**ichthyosaurs** A group of extinct reptiles that were adapted for life in water. They were abundant for much of the Mesozoic Era.

**iguanodonts** Herbivorous dinosaurs that included hadrosaurs and were widespread and very varied during the Cretaceous Period.

**invertebrate** An animal without a backbone.

**lambeosaurines** Hadrosaurs that had nasal passages that extended into the crests on the top of their heads. They included *Lambeosaurus*.

**ligament** A tough band of tissue that holds together internal organs and connects bones in an animal or human body.

**lungfish** Air-breathing fish that have one or two lungs.

**mammals** Warm-blooded vertebrates in which the young are fed with milk from the mother's mammary glands.

**maniraptors** A group that includes dinosaurs such as therizinosaurs and oviraptors, as well as birds.

**marsupial** An animal that carries its young in a pouch, such as a kangaroo.

**megafauna** A term describing the gigantic animals that flourished during the Pleistocene Epoch.

**membrane** A thin layer of tissue that is often tightly stretched.

**meteorite** A natural object from space, such as a piece of rock, that hits Earth's surface.

**molluscs** A large group of invertebrate animals that includes snails and slugs, as well as squid and octopuses.

**mosasaurs** A group of extinct reptiles that flourished in the world's seas and oceans after the extinction of the ichthyosaurs and the decline of the plesiosaurs.

**neural spine** Part of the vertebrae that, in some dinosaurs, became stretched into tall spines that held up sails or humps of fat on their backs.

**nutrients** Vital substances obtained from food and needed for growth.

**omnivore** An organism that obtains its nutrients both from plants and other vegetation and from eating meat.

**organism** A life form; a living being.

**Ornithischia** One of the two main orders of dinosaurs (the other being Saurischia), based on the evolution of the hip bones into a bird-like hip structure. Birds themselves, however, are part of the order Saurischia.

**ossify** To harden like bone.

**oviraptors** Small theropod dinosaurs found in Mongolia. They included *Oviraptor* and *Caudipteryx*.

**palaeontologist** A scientist who studies prehistoric life: for example, fossilized remains.

**phylogenetic tree** A diagram that shows the evolutionary relationships between species or groups of species.

**placoderms** Early armoured fish.

**plesiosaurs** A group of extinct reptiles that were adapted for life in water.

**pliosaurs** Any of the short-necked plesiosaurs, such as *Liopleurodon*.

**predator** Any organism that hunts other organisms (its prey) for food.

**pterosaurs** Flying reptiles in which the forelimbs had evolved to create wings. They lived in the Mesozoic Era.

**quadruped** An animal that moves about on four limbs.

**reptiles** Amniote vertebrates that have scales covering their bodies. There are many extinct groups of reptiles, including the dinosaurs.

**rhamphorhynchoids** Pterosaurs that had beaked snouts, pointed teeth and a long tail ending in a diamond-shaped flap of skin.

**rhynchocephalians** Reptiles that looked very similar to lizards.

**Saurischia** One of the two main orders of dinosaurs (the other being Ornithischia), based on the evolution of the hip bones into a lizard-like hip structure. Birds belong to this order.

**sauropodomorphs** A group of long-necked, herbivorous dinosaurs that included *Plateosaurus*.

**species** In biology, a way of classifying a group of organisms that share characteristics and are capable of breeding with each other to produce healthy offspring.

**spinal cord** In vertebrates, the long bundle of nerves that connects the brain with the rest of the body.

**stegosaurs** A group of large herbivorous armoured dinosaurs that included *Stegosaurus*.

**supercontinent** A single large land mass.

**tendon** A tough band of tissue that usually connects muscle to bone.

**tetrapod** A vertebrate with four limbs.

**therapsids** Mammal-like reptiles that include some ancestors of mammals.

**therizinosaurs** Dinosaurs that were originally meat-eaters but then turned into herbivores.

**theropods** A group of mainly carnivorous dinosaurs that included *Tyrannosaurus rex*.

**thorax** In an organism, the middle region of the body between the head and the stomach.

**titanosaurs** A group of extremely large sauropod dinosaurs that included the biggest and heaviest creatures ever to walk on Earth, such as *Argentinosaurus*.

**USSR** The Union of Soviet Socialist Republics, a communist state that existed between 1922 and 1991.

**vertebrae** The bones that form the backbone or spine.

**vertebrate** An organism with a backbone.

**warm-blooded** Describes animals in which the body temperature remains roughly constant and is controlled internally.

# Index